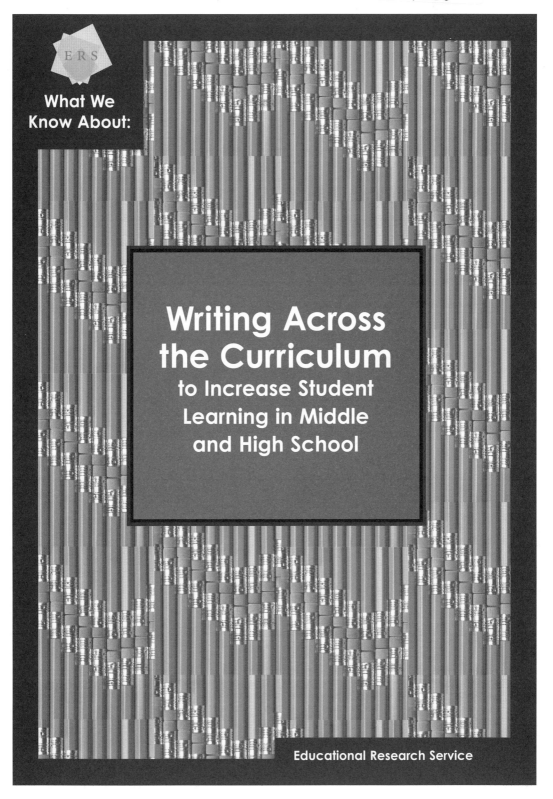

ERS

What We Know About:

Writing Across the Curriculum
to Increase Student Learning in Middle and High School

Educational Research Service

Because research and information make the difference.

Educational Research Service
1001 North Fairfax Street, Suite 500, Alexandria, VA 22314-1587
Tel: (703) 243-2100 or (800) 791-9308
Fax: (703) 243-1985 or (800) 791-9309
Email: ers@ers.org • Web site: www.ers.org

Educational Research Service is the nonprofit organization serving the research and information needs of the nation's K-12 education leaders and the public. Founded by seven national school management associations, ERS provides quality, objective research and information that enable local school district administrators to make the most effective school decisions, both in terms of day-to-day operations and long-range planning. Refer to the last page of this publication to learn how you can benefit from the services and resources available through an annual ERS Subscription.

ERS offers a number of research-based resources that particularly complement this report on writing in the middle and high school grades. Please refer to the Order Form at the back of this publication for a listing of some of these materials. Alternatively, visit us online at www.ers.org for a more complete overview of the wealth of K-12 research and information products and services available through ERS.

ERS Founding Organizations:

American Association of School Administrators
American Association of School Personnel Administrators
Association of School Business Officials International
National Association of Elementary School Principals
National Association of Secondary School Principals
National School Public Relations Association

Ordering information: Additional copies of *Writing Across the Curriculum to Increase Student Learning in Middle and High School* may be purchased at the base price of $20.00 each (ERS Comprehensive subscriber price: $10.00; ERS Individual subscriber price: $15.00). Quantity discounts available. Stock No. 0558. ISBN 1-931762-35-X.

Order from: Educational Research Service, 1001 North Fairfax Street, Suite 500, Alexandria, VA 22314-1587. Telephone: (800) 791-9308. Fax: (800) 791-9309. Email: ers@ers.org. Web site: www.ers.org. Add the greater of $4.50 or 10% of total purchase price for postage and handling. Phone orders accepted with Visa, MasterCard, or American Express.

ERS Management Staff:

John M. Forsyth, Ph.D., President and Director of Research
Katherine A. Behrens, Chief Operating Officer
Kathleen McLane, Chief Knowledge Officer

Authors:

Elizabeth Shellard, Senior Research Specialist, with Nancy Protheroe, Director of Special Research Projects.

Contents

Foreword vii

Chapter One:
Writing at the Middle and High School Levels 1
   Writing to Support Content-Area Learning 3
   Establishing a Strong Foundation for Writing Instruction 5

Chapter Two:
Learning to Read and Learning to Write—
Two Complementary Processes 7
   Emergent Literacy 8
   Reading and Writing as Interrelated Processes 9
   Stages of Writing Development 10
      Emergent Writing 11
      Beginning Writing 11
      Fluent Writing 12
   Effective Literacy Instruction 12
      Developing Students' Motivation to Read and Write 13

Chapter Three:
Teaching Writing—The Fundamentals 17
   What Does Instruction that Supports Student Writing Look Like? 18
   The Process Approach to Teaching Writing 22
      Prewriting 24
      Drafting 24
      Editing and Revising 24
      Publishing 26
   Helping Students Develop Purpose and Ideas for Their Writing 26
   Writing for an Audience 29
   Teaching the Mechanics of Writing 30

Chapter Four:
Strategies for Writing to Learn 33
   Writing as a Pre-Reading Activity 35
      Previewing Texts 36

   Free Writes 36

   Admit/Exit Slips 37

  Journal Writing 38

   Dialogue Journals 42

   Reciprocal Teaching Journals 44

  Learning Logs 45

  Reflective Writing 48

  Integrating Writing and Cooperative Learning 50

  Other Strategies for Using Writing to Promote Learning 51

  In Summary 55

Chapter Five:

Writing in Mathematics, Science, and Social Studies 57

  Using Writing in Mathematics Classes 57

  Using Writing in Science Classes 61

  Using Writing in Social Studies Classes 62

Chapter Six:

Assessment of Student Writing:

Purposes, Approaches, and Tools 67

  Why Assess Student Writing? 67

  Assessment as a Meaning-Making Process 69

  Using Rubrics to Assess Student Writing 70

   6+1 Traits of Student Writing 71

   Other Rubrics for Writing 73

   Involving Students in Developing Criteria Charts 74

Chapter Seven:

Helping Struggling Writers 79

  Making the Writing Experience Less Threatening 82

  Some Common Problems 83

  Addressing the Mechanics of Writing 85

   Using Technology to Support Students 85

  Helping Students Learn How to Evaluate Their Own Work 86

Chapter Eight:

Taking a Schoolwide Approach 91

References 99

Index 105

About the Authors

Elizabeth Shellard is senior research specialist at Educational Research Service. She has authored several articles and books on literacy instruction, the teaching of writing, principal leadership, and the characteristics of effective schools. She holds an M.Ed. in Curriculum and Instruction and is a former elementary classroom teacher.

Nancy Protheroe is director of special research projects at Educational Research Service. She has 25 years' experience coordinating the research and writing of projects such as the ERS *What We Know About* series and reference guides for principals and superintendents. Her areas of specialization include instructional technology, school finance, special education, and characteristics of successful classrooms, schools, and districts.

Foreword

Educational Research Service is pleased to publish this *What We Know About: Writing Across the Curriculum to Increase Student Learning in Middle and High School*. The report discusses the importance of effective writing instruction from two perspectives. First, communication skills, including writing, are becoming increasingly important. The National Commission on Writing in America's Schools and Colleges characterizes "writing today [as] not a frill for the few, but an essential skill for the many." Second, it highlights the positive impact writing can have in helping students learn content-area skills and knowledge.

The past few years have seen unprecedented activity focused on middle-level and high school education. Professional associations, foundations, the federal government, and state departments of education—as well as local school districts—all have been involved in efforts to identify ways to improve middle and high school education. While the projects take different approaches, all have one goal—improving student achievement—as a foundation.

However, substantially—and rapidly—improving student achievement is proving to be more difficult at the middle and high school levels than in elementary schools. Thus, educators working in these schools need approaches that are both effective and make efficient use of instructional time. This *What We Know About* demonstrates that embedding writing instruction, as well as opportunities to write, in all content-area classes is one such approach.

Too few secondary-level teachers, however, had courses focused on writing instruction during preservice training or staff development. This report was written to provide these teachers with a conceptual background, instruct them in key elements of good writing instruction, and, perhaps most important, provide specific suggestions for how to provide opportunities for writing that reinforce the learning of content-area skills.

As with other reports in the *What We Know About* series, the context for the discussion is provided by research findings, informed opinions contained in the professional literature, and examples from school personnel of "what works." Topics addressed in this publication include: the fundamentals of teaching writing; strategies for using writing to learn; use of writing in mathematics, science, and social studies classes; assessment of student writing; ways to help struggling writers; and the role schools can play in supporting student and teacher efforts.

Writing Across the Curriculum to Increase Student Learning in Middle and High School is written for practitioners—for teachers, school administrators, curriculum specialists, and staff development personnel—who want to begin using or expand the use of writing as an important tool for increasing student learning across the content areas. ERS hopes this publication will help individual teachers and entire schools with their efforts.

John M. Forsyth, Ph.D.
President and Director of Research

Chapter One

Writing at the Middle and High School Levels

Writing is a fundamental skill—it enables individuals to record and reflect on their experiences, share ideas, and preserve and transmit information across generations. Most individuals engage in writing activities every day—they write letters, make lists, fill out applications, and jot down notes. Given the important function of writing in society, the improvement of students' writing skills should be a significant focus of school curricula from the early elementary grades through high school and college. While this focus exists in the elementary grades, however, writing instruction often receives too little attention in middle and high school content-area classes.

In many middle and high schools, writing is a skill practiced almost exclusively in language arts and English classes because teachers in other subject areas are focused on teaching content-area information and skills identified by state and district standards. Frequently, these teachers may feel there is not enough time to teach writing because their students will face a high-stakes content-area test in the spring. In addition, many content-area teachers feel unprepared to teach and assess writing because they have received little training in the area.

But there is an increasing realization that students need both more time and more varied opportunities for writing. In response, many states have developed standards for writing proficiency and have begun to include writing components on their standardized tests. The Wisconsin Department of Public Instruction offers this rationale for its development of academic standards for writing:

> The rationale for the need for a strong emphasis on writing skills for our students is that written communication skills are central to learning. Whether in academic life, in the workplace, or in personal life, these skills offer a powerful advantage in a world in which people must constantly learn and use new information. To become confident and effective

writers, students need to learn how to write for various purposes and audiences. They need to try different approaches and to reconsider what they have written through revision and editing. To ensure that their writing is understood and well-received, students need a working knowledge of language as well as the rules and skills of grammatical structures, diction and usage, spelling, layout, and presentation. This knowledge is also invaluable for discussing, critiquing, revising, and editing written communication in almost any form (1998, online).

The results of the 2002 National Assessment of Educational Progress support this need for an increased focus on improving students' writing. Data collected from the assessment show too many students at the fourth-, eighth-, and 12th-grade levels have mastered only the basics of writing (Persky, Daane, and Jin 2003). In addition, findings suggest "only about one-quarter at each grade level are at or above the 'proficient' level…. [and that students] cannot systematically produce writing at the high levels of skill, maturity, and sophistication required in a complex, modern economy" (National Commission on Writing in America's Schools and Colleges 2003, 16). The problem is not that students do not know how to write, but rather that they do not know how to write with the skill expected of them today (National Commission on Writing in America's Schools and Colleges 2003).

Another reason to provide increased opportunities for student writing is related to the change in reading expectations as students move through the grades. At the elementary level, reading instruction focuses primarily on learning to read. In the upper grades, however, students are expected to read to learn, and the reading material required becomes more difficult. To ensure understanding of what they are reading, students should be asked to respond to this reading material—to produce their own analysis of the content, to evaluate its argument or position, and to formulate their own position statements on the topic. Students also need to know how to outline and organize their ideas in a coherent and persuasive manner. By engaging in different types of writing, they can better understand different types of reading material. For example, an assignment requiring a student to take a point of view and write a persuasive argument better prepares him to be a critical reader.

Finally, students in middle and especially high school should be developing competencies that will help them achieve success in their post-high school years. Writing skills are an important asset for students attending college. For those who go directly to the workforce, a baseline expectation of business is that graduates "can write clearly for a variety of purposes . . . since

English Language Arts Standards

Analysis of the National Council of Teachers of English/International Reading Association *Standards for English Language Arts* and standards documents from California, Colorado, Delaware, Maryland, Massachusetts, Michigan, New York, Oregon, Texas, and Vermont reveals remarkable similarities. Although the documents are organized in very different ways with somewhat different purposes, consensus prevails.

- While state standards documents often discuss reading and writing in separate standards, all documents center on the guiding principle that reading and writing must be taught together. This integration is stressed to the extent that all ten state documents studied emphasize the integration of the English language arts.

- Both national and state standards emphasize the importance of writing for a variety of purposes and a variety of audiences. All recommend the use of a writing process. Although they differ in the terms they use to describe accepted practices in spoken or written English, all language arts standards documents reviewed reflect the importance of adhering to language conventions. The documents regard the mastery of conventions as a vehicle for controlling ideas and enhancing understanding, and they place emphasis on correct usage, mechanics, sentence structure, paragraph structure, and sentence variety. In some state documents, these conventions include formatting and legibility (American Council on Education 1999, 3).

communication skills (written, verbal, and symbolic) are increasingly important in all categories of employment" (Vermont Business Roundtable 1995, online).

Writing to Support Content-Area Learning

To assist middle and high school students in becoming proficient writers, the National Commission on Writing in America's Schools and Colleges suggests the time provided for students to write be doubled and this additional time be found by providing opportunities to write "across the curriculum" (2003, 28). To many content-area teachers struggling with the need to cover an already jam-packed curriculum, this might seem impractical or even unrealistic. But both research and practice support the notion that using writing as a tool in these classes can do double duty—it can provide opportunities for writing while simultaneously strengthening student understanding of the information and skills being taught. The Commission notes:

> If students are to make knowledge their own, they must struggle with the details, wrestle with the facts, and rework raw information and dimly understood concepts into language they can communicate to someone else. In short, if students are to learn, they must write (2003, 9).

"How do I know what I think until I see what I say?" Forster's rhetorical question ... [presents] writing itself as an act of thinking. There's something about the very act of scribbling words down on a notepad, or tapping them into a computer, that draws ideas out and causes writers to make connections and flash on insights they never thought of before (Boise State Writing Center 2003, online).

Content-area teachers who already use writing as a tool have discovered its power in helping students to better grasp and retain concepts. Math teacher Joan Countryman describes a classroom experience:

> "Does your answer make sense?" I asked an algebra student who had come to me for extra help with his homework. The question seemed to startle him. We looked at each other, the tenth-grader and the first-year math teacher, and his eyes told me that it had not occurred to him that any of it should make sense. That moment was to shape my career as a teacher of mathematics. It challenged me to find ways to help students see the meaning in the math that they were learning. Writing about the homework, explaining the graphs and functions, making up word problems, and producing biographies of important mathematicians proved to be powerful tools (2001, online).

She describes the student's attempts to understand operations with integers. After he wrote a description of what he had noticed about adding integers—which he understood—and subtracting integers—which confused him—

Countryman wrote back with suggestions of another way to think about it. He added to his writing, and in Countryman's words, "You can almost hear Gary thinking as you read his description" (2001, online). The process of putting the abstract concept into words was a meaning-making activity for him.

An overview of writing in social studies includes additional teacher support for the approach:

> Social studies educators have produced a body of experientially based literature justifying and applying writing as an instructional tool in teaching social studies.

> This rationale posits at least three important benefits for students. The first is that writing stimulates higher-order thinking as students necessarily assemble, evaluate, select or discard, organize, and relate facts, concepts, and generalizations in the act of composing. Such manipulation of data is at the heart of learning. A second benefit is that out of this manipulation of data comes a realization of new relationships and new insights, hence the generation of students' new knowledge. Finally, a third benefit is that students must grapple with the effects of point of view—the writer's and the reader's—and in so doing come to better appreciate the role of perspective in creating and interpreting.

> Most of what students now write in social studies classrooms is for the purpose of evaluation. They compose products to demonstrate to the teacher what they have already "learned." Both research and practice now suggest that carefully designed writing tasks can in fact generate learning itself. Successful teachers have students write for both reasons (Maryland Department of Education n.d., online).

Without argument, most teachers would agree that "a central purpose of their instruction is to help students understand something significant about their content area" (Jacobs 2002, 58). Once teachers recognize the many ways in which writing can contribute to and enhance student understanding of content-area instruction, they may be more willing to teach the skills necessary for effective writing (Jacobs 2002).

Establishing a Strong Foundation for Writing Instruction

Teaching writing is a complex task. While content-area teachers may understand the importance of helping students express their ideas clearly in written form, they may be unsure of the best methods for helping students develop proficiency. Some may wonder how they can use writing to help their students better grasp content-area material. Or they may ask, "What can I do to make this report or writing assignment more interesting?" High school teachers may wonder whether the process approach to writing used in many elementary schools is appropriate for use with their students. Or they may be concerned with how to help students who have difficulty expressing their ideas clearly in written form.

It is not uncommon for writing tasks to produce anxiety in both teachers and students. Take a moment and put yourself in the shoes of your students and free write on a topic of your choosing for the next 10 minutes. As you reflect on your writing, consider these questions: Did you have trouble choosing a topic to write about? Were you able to write for the whole 10 minutes? Did you find yourself revising as you were writing? Were you concerned about grammar and punctuation? What would you have done differently, if anything, if you had known your writing would be read by someone else?

Undertaking this common classroom task yourself can be an eye-opening experience that provides insight into why so many students complain of "not having anything to write about." The indecision associated with choosing a writing topic, combined with the stress of requirements for correct spelling, punctuation, and grammar, instills a sense of fear in many students when they are asked to write. Completing this free-write activity may be a valuable professional development exercise for school instructional staff because it helps adults to understand the anxiety students may feel when asked to complete an open-ended writing assignment.

The first step to becoming an effective teacher of writing is becoming comfortable with one's own ability to write. All too often teachers feel inhibited when it comes to writing words down on paper, or they just don't have opportunities for it in their daily lives. Many view writing as a chore, something to be worked at, and something they do not enjoy. If this is a teacher's attitude toward writing, it likely will be passed on to the teacher's students. Conversely, a teacher who shows a genuine enthusiasm for writing, excitement for literary activities, and effectively models writing is more likely to instill a positive attitude toward writing in students.

Both research and practice are helping to identify ways to teach writing and to help struggling writers. Knowledge of this information can help teachers learn how to motivate and inspire students to write, plan, and effectively integrate writing into content-area instruction.

Chapter Two

Learning to Read and Learning to Write—Two Complementary Processes

If middle and high school teachers are to effectively help their students develop as writers, they need to understand how students develop literate behaviors and learn to read and write. For many of these teachers, this information was not provided in preservice classes, and it is unlikely that it is addressed in professional development provided for them. This chapter provides some of this basic information, thus providing a context for writing instruction in content-area classes.

Research into the relationship between reading and writing shows that those who read well often also write well (Smith and Dahl 1984). This phenomenon has been explained in several ways. It has been suggested that writing contributes to a reader's sense of the author's craft and of the strengths and weaknesses of literary works (Tierney and Leys 1986). In addition, both skilled reading and writing have been linked to reflective behaviors and metacognitive awareness (Birnbaum 1986).

Strong et al. propose that writing improves reading skills for the following five reasons:

- Writing involves reading what we've written and asking questions about its strengths.

- Writing about reading naturally makes us more reflective as we work to determine essential information and connect what we read to our lives.

- Writing leads us through the same process that writers go through in creating the texts we read.

- Writing gives us a deep, hands-on perspective on structure and technique as we work both consciously and unconsciously to produce more reader-friendly texts.

- Writing helps us organize our responses to reading (2002, 135).

The term writing actually refers to a variety of activities. In-school writing might mean any of the following: writing a summary of a book chapter, expressing oneself in a dialogue journal, writing an essay, editing a peer's work, or developing a word problem in math. Moreover, writing can be integrated with reading in several ways. Writing might be a pre-reading activity (such as jotting down associations with the Renaissance before reading about it) or a post-reading activity (such as analyzing the structure of a poem).

Emergent Literacy

Many children seem to develop reading and writing skills almost effortlessly. This is especially true for children who have been read to routinely through their preschool years. Some middle and high school students, however, may not have had the support they needed during their preschool and elementary years to develop important foundational skills. Understanding this, content-area teachers might be better able to provide appropriate instruction for these struggling students.

Until the 1970s, it was believed that five-year-olds entered kindergarten to be "readied" for reading and writing instruction, which was to begin in first grade—a theory known as "reading readiness." Age six was viewed as the "magic" year in which a flip could be switched to trigger literacy development in children.

We now know this is not the case, however, and there is no "magic" age at which children are ready to learn to read and write. Research shows children begin developing literacy skills gradually throughout their preschool years. When students enter kindergarten, most are able to recognize signs, logos, and other forms of environmental print. In addition, many already are able to retell stories and scribble "letters" in an attempt at writing and know how to hold a book and turn the pages. Some have even taught themselves how to read.

This perspective on how children learn to read and write is known as "emergent literacy," a term coined by New Zealand educator Marie Clay. It recognizes that children gain literacy skills beginning as young as 12 months by listening to stories, watching as adults read and write, scribbling letters, and observing environmental print. Teale and Sulzby describe young children's literacy development in this way:

- Children begin to read and write very early in life.

- Young children learn the functions of literacy through observing and participating in real-life settings in which reading and writing are used.

- Young children's reading and writing abilities develop concurrently and inter-relatedly through experiences in reading and writing.

- Young children learn through active involvement with literacy materials, by constructing their understanding of reading and writing (in Tompkins 1998, 138).

According to the emergent literacy perspective, literacy skills develop best in a natural environment in which children are exposed to oral language, able to observe adults reading and writing, provided with crayons for scribbling, and encouraged to handle books. This perspective assumes children are active learners who construct their own knowledge about reading and writing from a very early age with the assistance of parents and others around them.

With the acceptance of the emergent literacy paradigm in kindergartens, the issue of when to begin formal literacy instruction has been resolved because the central tenet of emergent literacy is that reading and writing development commences long before children even reach kindergarten (Teale and Yakota 2000). The question now is not when to begin literacy instruction, but how.

Reading and Writing as Interrelated Processes

Reading and writing are meaning-making processes that often develop simultaneously. Teale and Yakota (2000) provide three reasons for integrating reading and writing instruction:

1) A particularly high relationship exists between phonics knowledge in reading and spelling ability.

2) As young children are encouraged to write using invented spelling, they build a concept of word and sound-symbol relationships.

3) Having children write makes it easier for them to learn to read.

As children write, they are also participating in several types of reading activities. For example, they may read works by other authors to gather ideas and learn about the structure of stories. They may also read and revise their own work as they attempt to clarify their own writing. Readers engage in many of the same activities that writers do, such as generating ideas, organizing, monitoring, problem solving, and revising. Additionally, both reading and writing are cyclical processes (Tompkins 1998).

To help students develop a clear concept of literacy and continue to grow as both readers and writers, Shanahan suggests teachers at *all* levels should:

- involve students in reading and writing experiences every day;

- plan instruction that reflects the developmental nature of the reading-writing relationship;

- make the reading-writing connection explicit to students;

- emphasize both the processes and the products of reading and writing;

- emphasize the purpose for which students use reading and writing; and

- teach reading and writing through meaningful, functional, and genuine literacy experiences (in Tompkins 1998, 132).

Stages of Writing Development

Through observation, children learn that the spoken word can be written down, that print carries meaning, and that reading and writing are used for a variety of purposes. From a very young age, children should be encouraged to "write." Their development in this area can be divided into three stages: emergent writing, beginning writing, and fluent writing.

Although it would seem at first glance that students at the middle and high school levels should have progressed far beyond the characteristics exhibited by young emergent writers, knowledge of this stage may provide direction for teachers working with struggling older writers. For example, teachers of very young children often assign picture drawing as a "writing" assignment. Middle and high school teachers whose classes include struggling writers occasionally might ask their students to use pictures or graphic structures to organize ideas. Such exercises can provide practice with organizing ideas—one of the elements of effective writing—and can then be used as a springboard for a writing assignment.

Emergent Writing

The first stage, emergent writing, is characterized by children's scribbles to represent writing. Scribbling is an important developmental step in the process of learning to write, as it signals a child's understanding that what he/she is thinking can be recorded. Encouraging students to read their "scribbles" reinforces for them that print has meaning and is something that can be translated into letter sounds.

During the emergent stage, children also should be encouraged to draw pictures. Murray writes, "If you ask young children to write a story, they are as likely to hand you drawings as bits of prose. They know instinctively . . . [that] writing is a visual art—writers see, then write" (2002, 58). In fact, young children's writing often grows out of talking and drawing (Tompkins 1998). Each picture a child draws tells a story—a story children should be encouraged to vocalize and possibly write down in words.

Beginning Writing

As children grow in their developmental literacy skills, they enter the beginning writing stage and begin to replace their scribbles with recognizable letters. Invented spelling is common in the writing of students at this stage and should be encouraged. Praise students' attempts to sound out words and to write down the letter sounds they hear. Their efforts reveal much about their understanding of letter-sound relationships and can be used to assess individual students' progress with early reading skills. As students grow as writers, they will gradually be expected to use conventional spelling in their writing, but this should not be an area of focus when students are in the beginning stage of writing.

Reading aloud with students and engaging in shared reading and writing activities will increase their understanding of literacy conventions and lead to gradual moves from invented to conventional spelling. At first, students' sentences may run together, but, with practice and exposure to printed texts, they will slowly learn to segment words and leave spaces between words. With time, students also will move from capitalizing random letters to using capital letters only at the beginning of a sentence and to begin proper nouns. Similarly, children gradually learn to use correct punctuation in their writing.

Fluent Writing

As students progress through the grades and become more proficient in using standard written conventions, the goal is for them to become fluent writers. The task of educators is to ensure students continue to exhibit the same enthusiasm for writing during this final stage that they showed in the early grades.

Recall how you felt when asked in the first chapter to free write on a topic of your choosing for 10 minutes. Chances are, you probably felt at least a little at a loss for what to write about. Many students experience this problem frequently, feeling that they have no significant experiences about which to write. By teaching students writing strategies, such as how to brainstorm, and by providing them choices in writing topics (with one always being "your choice"), teachers can help students overcome the anxiety that choosing a topic may produce. Allowing students to write in less-structured time frames also can increase their motivation to write and their enjoyment of the activity (Gutman and Sulzby 2001).

As students move through these stages, they need to be reassured that their writing does not need to be "perfect." All too often, students feel the need to spell all of their words accurately—a belief that will lead some of them to view writing as a tedious, frustrating activity. Tompkins (1998) stresses the need to contrast teachers' writing—adult writing—with the "kid" writing that children can do. She writes, "Kid writing is important for young children to understand because it gives them permission to experiment with written language when they draw and write. Too often children assume that they should write and spell like adults do, and they cannot" (170). Without this understanding of "kid writing," students will be tempted to ask adults to spell every word for them or to copy text out of books or from charts.

Effective Literacy Instruction

Thus, it is clear that effective literacy instruction begins with a language-rich environment that maximizes students' motivation to read and write. In addition, this focus should be consciously and explicitly maintained by middle and high school teachers. When the classroom is seen as a place where oral and written language are highly valued, students are more likely to be motivated to excel in literacy-related activities.

Langer and Flihan suggest "students do best with frequent and extended opportunities to read and write . . . and when exposed to a body of literature that represents a variety of genres, topics, and styles" (2000, online). The researchers also mention students should be provided with choice in what they read and write, as the opportunity to read and write about topics of interest positively affects student attitudes toward learning.

In addition, research has shown students learn best when the learning context is varied to include cooperative learning groups, small and large group instruction, and buddy partnering (Hiebert 1991). Teachers should provide students with opportunities within each of these instructional contexts to consider their personal responses to texts they read and compose and to make links between their prior experiences and what they are reading and writing (Langer and Flihan 2000).

Developing Students' Motivation to Read and Write

Motivation is a critical factor underlying literacy success. When schools encourage students' motivation to read and write by making the processes enjoyable and tailored to their interests, the students are more likely to evolve into lifelong readers and writers.

A four-year study of the factors influencing students' motivation found that when students had opportunities for authentic self-expression in language arts activities, they were more highly motivated. Moreover, students interviewed as part of the study reported that they experienced the highest levels of motivation when they had ownership over the learning activities. Specific activities they mentioned included opportunities to:

- express their own ideas and opinions;

- choose topics for writing and books for reading;

- talk about books they were reading;

- share their writings with classmates; and

- pursue "authentic" activities—not worksheets—using the language arts (Oldfather 1995).

Merritt provides additional information on aspects of assignments that can help to build student interest in and motivation about writing; for example, students tend to enjoy:

- requests to use an atypical genre (for example, using narrative writing in science);

- a sense of challenge;

- a feeling that the writing can actually make a difference, cause a change, or be enjoyed by real people;

- opportunities for meaningful collaboration; and

- use of multimedia and technology tools (Merritt 2003, 28).

Research on student motivation stresses the need to emphasize students' intrinsic motivation to read and write, but also recognizes that outside sources may be needed to fuel and sustain student interest. Above all else, student motivation is dependent on students' feelings of being competent and in control. The role of the teacher should be the development of a classroom environment that helps students to experience these feelings by ensuring they have opportunities to engage in developmentally appropriate tasks, by offering instructional support, and by encouraging students to internalize what they have learned. Collaborative activities in which students work with others often provide support and less perceived risk. Scaffolding of student instruction is another means of ensuring that students move from easy to more challenging tasks in ways that allow them to retain control and independence during the learning process while teacher support is provided when needed (Strickland, Ganske, and Monroe 2002).

Many teachers also increase students' motivation to write by engaging them in authentic, meaningful writing tasks. For example, English teacher David McKay, the Washington State English Teacher of the Year, challenges his students to publish a book each year. Reed explains:

> Frustrated with his inability to get all his students motivated to do their best work, [McKay] decided to try something different: a year-long project to research, write, publish, and sell an entire book (23). McKay says, "I needed an assignment that would take students to a higher level.... Being published is attractive to many students. They buy into the idea that they are making books—something that will last a long time, be found in homes and local libraries, be read by people they know. It challenges them to raise their standards to another level" (2002, 23).

During the first year of the project, McKay's students researched and collected oral histories on the tradition of the Thanksgiving Day football game between their town and a neighboring village. The students interviewed parents, families, and community members who had graduated from either high school since 1906 (the year the tradition began), read old newspapers, and collected old photographs. McKay then chose one 11th-grade English class to compile and edit all the materials into a professional quality manuscript. Once this was completed, McKay sent the manuscript to a local publishing company and ordered 1,000 copies. To everyone's surprise, the book sold out quickly, and sales added up to twice the investment for printing.

McKay continues to be awed by his students' excitement and motivation to publish a book each year, but he also understands why students are eager to participate. He says:

> It's clearly more difficult and challenging for the students than just writing papers.... They understand that the stakes are high. Because publishing is permanent, accuracy and correctness are extremely important. Almost all of them rise to the challenge, and some go farther—they discover that they are writers and have something to offer other people. They are extremely proud to be published authors, and they learn a great deal about how writing can affect people's lives (in Reed 2002, 24).

Through these yearlong writing projects, McKay is able to engage his students in the writing process, build vocabulary, teach grammar, hold writing workshops, and encourage collaboration and cooperation among students. Their high level of motivation to write—and write well—provides strong support for their learning of the skills identified in the state's standards.

Chapter Three

Teaching Writing—The Fundamentals

Even content-area teachers who agree they should incorporate writing instruction in their classrooms may struggle with practical aspects—the how-to's. They may wonder how to help their students contend with issues of audience, purpose, clarity, style, genre, punctuation, spelling, and handwriting. And they may wonder how to assist their students in getting from point A, the selection of a topic, to point B, the development of a draft, to point C, the finished product.

Some general elements of effective writing instruction—for example, structuring assignments in ways that increase student motivation—have already been discussed in the previous chapter. Research over the past 20 years, however, has identified important additional information about what good writing instruction looks like. This chapter discusses key elements of that information and so provides direction for content-area teachers.

In addition, the chapter includes a discussion of the fundamentals of writing instruction from the perspective of the process approach to writing—one that involves steps such as drafting and revising. Knowing about these components of effective writing instruction will enable content-area teachers to help their students become better writers within all disciplines. It also is important to note however, that many of the writing opportunities that can be provided in content-area classes will be less formal than research papers or essays and will not require the multiple steps described in the process approach. Merritt clarifies this in her response to the question, "Does all writing have to end with a final, published work?":

> Writing can be done for many different purposes, only some of which culminate in a final, published work. In fact, writing can be used as a tool for learning, not just showing what was learned, in all disciplines (2003, 14).

She provides collaborative note-taking as an example. In this activity, students read a section of the text, individually write down the main points, discuss these with other students, and then add the information they missed to their notes. Merritt also expands on the everyday use of the writing process:

> Terms such as "prewriting," "drafting," "revising," "editing," and "publishing" are often used to refer to stages in the process, but it is important to remember that not all pieces of writing will go through every part of the process and that the process tends to be recursive (moving back and forth among the parts of the process) rather than linear (starting with prewriting and moving straight through each part of the process in isolation). Writers may find themselves editing while drafting, using prewriting activities to develop their ideas in the middle of the composition, or revising and editing simultaneously. In fact, individual students will differ in their writing processes, and even the same student may use different processes for different assignments. As a result, there is no one "process" that all writing should go through or that every teacher should use with every assignment. However, the following explanations and suggestions may be useful during particular stages of the writing process (2003, 4).

What Does Instruction that Supports Student Writing Look Like?

While many teachers may point to a lack of a focus on writing instruction in their own preservice preparation as a barrier to providing support for their students, research on the teaching of writing provides clear direction about what is important. For example, it is important that students write every day. In addition, effective writing instruction:

- uses a basic framework of planning, writing, and revision;
- instructs students in the steps, features, and conventions of the writing process; and
- provides feedback aligned with what was explicitly taught (Warger 2002).

Researchers from the National Research Center on English Learning and Achievement provide additional information about "what works" in writing instruction, based on five years of classroom observations. The researchers studied:

> English programs in two sets of middle and high schools with similar student populations. In one set of schools, students "beat the odds" and

Characteristics of Classrooms that Support Writing Instruction

Graham identifies the following characteristics of classrooms that provide high-quality writing instruction:

- frequent opportunities for students to write;

- students working on the same piece of writing over time;

- students writing for multiple audiences on real writing tasks and sharing their efforts with classmates;

- teachers encouraging children to think, reflect, and revise as they write;

- a classroom environment where students help each other and in which the teacher is encouraging and supportive of their efforts;

- instructional support aimed at helping students grow or progress as writers;

- a reasonable balance with regard to emphasis on meaning versus form;

- teachers who like to write and share their writing with students;

- the use of reading and other language skills to support the development of writing, and vice versa; and

- an orientation that reading and writing are not separate; rather, they are important and reciprocal components of literacy (1992, 134).

outperform their peers on high-stakes, standardized tests of English skills and read and write at high levels of proficiency. In the other set of schools, students perform more typically…. By comparing these two sets of classrooms, [the researchers] have been able to identify and validate six features of instruction that make a difference in student performance (Langer with Close, Angelis, and Preller 2000, 2).

One of these features is particularly relevant to a discussion of integrating opportunities for writing in content-area instruction. Teachers in the high-performing schools use a variety of teaching approaches to help students learn particular skills and information. Specifically, while the students might first be presented with the information in a lesson "without considering its larger use or meaning" (2), the teachers would then follow up with "integrated" activities. For example, one teacher has her students develop analogies and then provide and discuss their rationales for each of them.

In addition, other researchers have found a link between the quality of writing assignments and the quality of student writing as evaluated by NAEP-type criteria. Eidman-Aadahl, Storms, and Gentile identified characteristics of strong writing assignments in four areas:

- **Content and Scope:** Successful writing assignments, the team found, are rooted in particular and substantive material. Students are required to interact with this material, transforming knowledge from different sources. So a successful assignment might ask students to read a story and compare the motivation of two characters. To execute this assignment, students would need to examine the characters and select information about each character for comparison, analyzing and transforming information from the story. By contrast, a weaker assignment might ask students to read a story and describe one of the characters. In this case, students are probably not working with the information; they are merely locating and restating it.

- **Organization and Development:** The researchers found that the best student writing occurs when assignments provide guidelines for how to structure ideas and writing with an appropriate level of scaffolding. Many common assignments do not provide this struc-ture…. [For example, the assignment], "Write a descriptive essay about a favorite place," gives no direction. The assignment is more likely to yield quality writing when it becomes more directive and complex: "Write a descriptive essay about a favorite place using the five senses," [which worked] in part because the teacher used it as a basis for a unit on descriptive sensory words.

- **Audience and Communication:** The better assignments asked students to write to an authentic audience in a genuine act of communi-cation. When the audience is not real and the communication not authentic, the writing is often weak. For instance, a typical eighth grade process paper asks students to write to the teacher explaining how to open a school locker. But the writer knows that the teacher—as well as everyone else in the school—already knows how to open a locker. The writing is a mere exercise. In its report, the team suggests another approach to a process paper. Ask students to identify an area of expertise (say tying fishing flies or collecting baseball cards) not shared by the reader and explain to that audience something about the activity using the writer's unique information or individual perspective.

- **Engagement and Choice:** The researchers found that students wrote best when assignments gave them the opportunity to become engaged. Engagement was most likely to occur when writers had a choice over features of their work such as topic, format (whether to write a letter or an essay, for instance), and audience. In one successful fourth grade assignment, students were asked to "Write an article giving tips on how to stay healthy, using facts from articles read in class." The students had read many articles that included information for many potential tips. The assignment offered choice about which hints to include. This choice seemed to contribute to the high degree of engagement found in the students' writing (in Peterson 2001, online).

Another way in which teachers can help students develop as writers is to make explicit connections between writing and the content-area knowledge base. Merritt discusses this:

Teachers can help [students] understand that, in many ways, writing is thinking, so they benefit from using it as a tool in other disciplines as well. One way teachers can show the importance of writing in the content area is to expose students to documents in the field that have had a profound influence on the direction of the discipline. For example, in science teachers can provide excerpts from works by scientists such as Einstein, Oppenheimer, and Copernicus. Another way is for teachers to identify some of the kinds of thinking that students need to be able to do in the content area and explicitly instruct students in how to use a variety of kinds of writing to help develop different kinds of thinking. For example, in geometry students need to be able to use logic to solve a problem, and writing analytically can help develop that skill. Another way is to have professionals in the field discuss the kinds of writing that are part of their job. Finally, teachers can engage students in meaningful writing activities in class as a way for them to "believe" in the power of writing as they see its purpose and benefits (2003, 27).

Merritt also suggests teachers provide students with opportunities to "analyze the characteristics of a particular genre of writing appropriate to the field"

(2003, 29). For example, students "can analyze ten different word problems in algebra and make a list of all of the features that they have in common before having to create their own original word problems" (29).

The Process Approach to Teaching Writing

Up to this point, this discussion about teaching writing has been general in nature. It has identified the importance of motivation, of providing opportunities for students to write, and of making explicit connections between writing and the needs of the content area. However, content-area teachers—even those teaching subject areas other than language arts or English—can provide more effective support for students who are learning to write if they better understand the process approach to teaching writing.

During the 1960s and 70s, process theorists took issue with the product-oriented approach to writing taken by most teachers. This product-oriented approach was characterized by:

> teachers [who] assigned papers, graded them, and then handed them back. They attended to the product—its clarity, originality, and correctness—but they did not attend to the writing process (Composition Center of Dartmouth College n.d., online).

In the view of these process theorists, "Writing is the result of a very complex, highly individualized process" (Composition Center of Dartmouth College, n.d., online), with the steps needed to produce a product as important as the product itself. They also felt that this writing process could be taught and so developed an instructional approach to teach specific steps in the process.

The writing process begins when an individual makes a decision to write, rather than when he/she takes out a pencil and begins writing, and concludes when the individual finishes writing. During this process, the individual moves through four stages: prewriting, drafting, editing/revising, and publishing.

Although the process approach is often used to teach writing in the elementary grades, it also is applicable for use at the middle and high school levels and can be done in tandem—with practice—with content-area instruction.

Elements of Effective Writing

Focus: Focus is the topic/subject established by the writer in response to the writing task. The writer must clearly establish a focus as he/she fulfills the assignment of the prompt. If the writer retreats from the subject matter presented in the prompt or addresses it too broadly, the focus is weakened. The writer may effectively use an inductive organizational plan which does not actually identify the subject matter at the beginning and may not literally identify the subject matter at all. The presence, therefore, of a focus must be determined in light of the method of development chosen by the writer. If the reader is confused about the subject matter, the writer has not effectively established a focus. If the reader is engaged and not confused, the writer probably has been effective in establishing a focus.

Organization: Organization is the progression, relatedness, and completeness of ideas. The writer establishes for the reader a well-organized composition, which exhibits a constancy of purpose through the development of elements forming an effective beginning, middle, and end. The writer establishes relationships between and among ideas and/or events throughout the response. The response demonstrates a clear progression of related ideas and/or events and is unified and complete.

Support and Elaboration: Support and elaboration is the extension and development of the topic/subject. The writer provides sufficient elaboration to present the ideas and/or events clearly. Two important concepts in determining whether details are supportive are the concepts of *relatedness* and *sufficiency*. To be supportive of the subject matter, details must be related to the focus of the response. Relatedness has to do with the directness of the relationship that the writer establishes between the information and the subject matter. Supporting details should be relevant and clear. The writer must present his/her ideas with enough power and clarity to cause the support to be sufficient. Effective use of concrete, specific details strengthens the power of the response. Insufficiency is often characterized by undeveloped details, redundancy, and the repetitious paraphrasing of the same point. Sufficiency has less to do with amount and more to do with the specificity and effectiveness of the support and elaboration provided.

Style: Style is the control of language that is appropriate to the purpose, audience, and context of the writing task. The writer's style is evident through word choice and sentence fluency. Skillful use of precise, purposeful vocabulary enhances the effectiveness of the composition through the use of appropriate words, phrases and descriptions that engage the audience. Sentence fluency involves using a variety of sentence styles to establish effective relationships between and among ideas, causes, and/or statements appropriate to the task.

Conventions: Conventions involve correctness in sentence formation, usage, and mechanics. The writer has control of grammatical conventions that are appropriate to the writing task. Errors, if present, do not impede the reader's understanding of the ideas conveyed (North Carolina Department of Public Instruction Testing Section 2003, 5-6).

Prewriting

During this initial stage of the writing process, students make decisions about what to write, why to write, which aspect of a topic to focus on, who their intended audience will be, and how they will approach the subject. Students should brainstorm ideas for writing assignments during this stage. Some students may use literature as models for their own writing, and this may be a good time for teachers to read aloud with students and model good writing while discussing elements such as writing style, topic, and audience. Trade books also show students how to approach a topic and how to focus on detail in describing events. Savage describes this stage as an "incubation time, a time to allow children's ideas to jell and take shape" (1998, 356).

Drafting

Students write their ideas on paper during the drafting stage of the writing process. This is a busy time—"details are reduced to words, key points to phrases. Thoughts are forged into sentences, and sentences are gathered into paragraphs" (Savage 1998, 356-57). While students are drafting, the classroom often acquires a workshop atmosphere. Student drafts will be in different stages, with some students just beginning to write, some midway through, and others nearly done with a draft. Teachers manage student progress at this stage by moving throughout the room, answering questions, and conferencing with individual students. The instructional needs that the teacher observes during this time may become mini-lesson topics. Problems with punctuation, run-on sentences, and subject-verb agreement are just a few of the common mistakes teachers observe (Savage 1998).

While working on their first drafts, students should be urged to simply get their ideas on paper without worrying about spelling, word usage, punctuation, or handwriting. Teachers and students can address the mechanics of writing during the editing and revision stages of the writing process.

Editing and Revising

Revision focuses on meaning and clarity. As students revise their work, they look to vary sentence structure and word choice, clarify ideas, elaborate upon undeveloped ideas, and delete unnecessary information. Savage describes the expectations for this stage: "At the revision stage, authors examine what they have written in comparison to the anticipated expectations of their readers; that is, they judge the 'fit' between what they have written and what they expect their readers to understand" (1998, 360).

Decisions in the Writing Process

Whether writing a fictional story in the second grade or a research paper in high school, the writing process consists of four stages, each of which involves a series of decisions.

Stages	Decisions
Prewriting	<ul><li>Stimulus for writing—*Why am I writing this?*</li><li>Finding a topic—*What will I write about?*</li><li>Focus on detail—*What aspect of the topic will I emphasize?*</li><li>Deciding on form—*Will I write a story or poem?*</li><li>Deciding on audience—*Who will read what I write?*</li></ul>
Drafting	<ul><li>Drafting—*What ideas and details will I include?*</li><li>Vocabulary—*What words will I use to express actions and feelings?*</li><li>Sentences—*How can I write so others will be interested and entertained?*</li></ul>
Editing/Revising	<ul><li>Sentences—*Do my sentences make sense? Are they clear? Do they begin with capitals and end with periods?*</li><li>Paragraphs—*Do they have topic sentences? Are they too long? Do I have enough ideas?*</li><li>Selection—*Does it have an interesting title? Did I include exciting action and interesting details?*</li></ul>
Publishing	<ul><li>Publishing—*Will it be a diary or journal for me only? Will it be shared with only select people such as parents or classmates? Will it be posted on a bulletin board or published in a class book? (Savage 1998, 365).*</li></ul>

Student-teacher and student-student conferences might occur during this stage of the writing process. Effective conferences focus on both the writing process and the product; accordingly, topics discussed during conferences should include where the writer got his/her idea for the piece, how he/she decided to approach the topic, and how the student might go about editing his/her work (Savage 1998). Fitzgerald (1989) also suggests that small group conferences can help students become better critical readers and writers. In this format, students take turns sharing their writing with the group, and students offer each author their comments, questions, and suggestions.

During the editing phase, students proofread their writing to ensure all words are spelled correctly, sentences are complete, and each sentence has correct capitalization and punctuation. Savage describes the editing phase as "more than a search for errors; it is a chance to help children develop an attitude of independent self-appraisal" (1998, 359). During this time, students take responsibility for improving their own writing.

Students need to know that these processes are a way to improve their writing and themselves as writers, and that this is a normal part of writing. Above all else, it is important for students to understand that editing and revising are not to be viewed as punishment for carelessness.

Publishing

Publication of students' writing is the final stage in the process approach to writing instruction and can take many forms. Students can read their writing aloud to the class, or they can hang their writing on a bulletin board in the classroom for students and visitors to read. Student writing also can be displayed in the hallways or published in the school newspaper or literary magazine.

Some teachers like to publish student writing in more formal ways—by binding it into a class book, making laminated covers for students' books, by stitching pages together, or by submitting writing samples to national literary magazines. In recent years, several Web sites have been developed devoted exclusively to publishing student writing. For example, the Merlyn's Pen Foundation (www.merlynspen.org/) supports teenaged writers through responding to writers who submit work for review and by posting fiction, poetry, and essays developed by teen writers.

Whatever form publication takes, it is important to treat these more formal student writing products as a form of literature. For many students, the publishing stage is the most exciting part of the literacy program and the writing process.

Helping Students Develop Purpose and Ideas for Their Writing

Choosing a writing topic can be a major stumbling block in the writing process for many students. All too often, teachers hear students say that they have "nothing to write about" or "don't know what to write about." To help a student choose a topic, some teachers will ask the students a series of questions, such as "What do you like to do in your free time?" "Tell me about your favorite vacation," or "Tell me about a time when you were scared."

For some students, the problem of choosing a topic stems from the fact that they don't view their own experiences as worthy writing topics. Teachers need to change this perception by encouraging students to tell their own stories. Literature can also help. For example, young adult literature often deals with experiences commonly encountered by teens, such as peer pressure, sports, or applying to college. By reading these selections, students learn that these events are worthy writing topics and that they can write their own stories on the topic.

Students also need to understand that writing serves a variety of purposes: to entertain, to persuade, to learn, to inform, and to evoke feelings. In order to help students understand the differences in these purposes, teachers should model writing and provide their students with guided, authentic practice in writing for a variety of purposes. The chart on the next page provides examples of possible writing activities that support writing aligned to each of these purposes.

Some teachers opt to provide students with writing prompts to help them develop ideas for their writing. These starters may be aligned with topics or units of study, or may be very general. For example, students who routinely participate in small-group activities in math class may be asked to respond to the following prompt as a wrap-up activity: What observations did your group make as you solved this problem?

Merritt provides some additional suggestions for helping students generate ideas for writing topics, all of which could be applied across content areas. For example:

- Students can be instructed to reread their notes from a particular unit with an eye toward "unanswered questions" that they could pursue to deepen their understanding of what they have been studying. Students can also be instructed to reread significant texts and mark them while reading to identify the ideas that seem most significant or intriguing to them.

- Students [are asked] . . . to write whatever comes to mind for ten minutes (can be about a particular topic or can be totally open). They are instructed to keep the pen or pencil moving the entire time and not to pause to "think" during the writing. If they draw a blank, they can write about how they can't think of anything to write about. Students then reread the freewriting for possible topic ideas that could be developed.

Purposes and Ideas for Writing	
Purpose for Writing	**General Description of Possible Writing Activities**
To entertain	• Create a new ending or beginning for the story • Retell the story in your own words • Create a parody of the prompt • Create a rhyme, poem, or patter based on the reading
To persuade	• Write a letter to one of the story's characters, giving advice or requesting help • Write a critical essay about the prompt • Write an editorial based on the prompt
To learn	• Retell an important event, process, or situation • Summarize or synthesize texts
To inform	• Report on a phenomenon mentioned in the text • Construct directions or instructions based on something that happens in the text • Describe and prepare a critique of the text
To evoke feelings	• Describe a personal experience that relates to the text • Give an account of what a character might think or feel • Create a journal or diary entry for a character • Write a letter to a story character or the author of the prompt (Farr 1993, 74).

- Students often benefit from simply having conversations about possible topics. For example, students can be put into groups of three and instructed to brainstorm ten words that they feel are significant to the content being covered in class. After making the list, they can discuss possible topics related to each word. They can also ask questions of each other in pairs to help elicit thinking about possible topics. Another way to use discussion is to engage students in seminar style discussions which can help them identify and articulate main ideas from a text that may become topics for writing.

- *Inspiration*, a software program designed especially to help develop ideas and organize thinking, can help students capture their ideas using an intuitive interface which focuses attention on thinking rather than technical issues.

- In pairs or small groups students "think through" writing ideas by using instant messaging or email to discuss where they want to go with their writing. Students may even be able to use some of this writing to "jump start" their brainstorming about the topic.

- Students are told to "dump" what they know about a topic in a ten-minute write. They then reread what they wrote and list three possible writing topics that could emerge from the dump (2003, 40).

Finally, routinely providing students with opportunities to write less formally, although with a focused purpose, can provide them with practice in making decisions about what to write without the pressure of looking ahead to a "big"—and so often challenging—final assignment.

Writing for an Audience

Writing is a method of communicating with an audience. Wildeman states, "No matter who/what the audience is (from real people to fictional constructs), writers adjust their discourse to their audiences. In other words, writers do things to bring their readers into their texts, to establish a community that includes themselves and their reader" (1988, 4).

Providing students with opportunities to understand—and to apply—the concept of audience is another aspect of effective writing instruction. For example, are they writing something to be shared with their classmates? Will their writing be graded by the teacher? Will the principal see their writing? Are they writing a letter to an elected official? Are they writing to a friend? Is it personal writing that will not be seen by anyone else?

All students can be taught to write with an audience in mind, if the teacher uses a wide range of audience-oriented teaching strategies that encourage students to write for a wide range of readers. Examples of such assignments include:

- *Letters to parents, friends, local community leaders, or sports figures.* Some teachers engage their students in letter exchanges with students in other classrooms or schools, while others choose to exchange letters with students themselves.

- *Stories or articles that will be "published."* When students know that their writing will be read by others, they are more aware of their audience and make a greater attempt to tailor their writing to their intended audience. Older students may appreciate having their writing published in the school newspaper or literary magazine, or even in a commercial magazine.

- *Assignments that will be shared with others.* Sharing their work with others gives students the opportunity to see if their audience gets the intended message or reacts in the intended manner. If students see that their audience is confused, they learn that they need to revise their writing to make it clearer for this particular audience (Strange 1988).

Teaching the Mechanics of Writing

Instruction in the mechanics of writing, often referred to under the umbrella term of "grammar," frequently includes instruction in punctuation, capitalization, and sentence structure. As students progress through the grades, it may also include information about parts of speech, parts of sentences, types of sentences, and usage. Research suggests grammar instruction is most effective when integrated with reading and writing instruction (Tompkins 1998).

Students learn much about the structure of the English language as they read. Authors use a variety of simple, compound, and complex sentence patterns, and often use rich, descriptive details to help their readers develop a mental image of a scene. Students pick up on these language patterns as they read and often strive to incorporate them into their own writing.

Teachers can plan mini-lessons on grammatical concepts by noting the type of usage and grammatical errors students are making. They may also identify mini-lesson topics by choosing a source that is particularly rich in a certain grammatical area—such as complex sentence structures—and discussing this sentence format with students. To help students practice writing more complex syntactic structures, some teachers choose to have students write new versions of patterned texts from books they are reading. Tompkins writes, "As they use the author's sentence forms to create new versions, students practice using more complex syntactic structures than they might normally use themselves" (1998, 526).

Research suggests that worksheets should not be used to teach grammatical concepts; rather, excerpts from books or from students' own writing should form the basis of instruction (Tompkins 1998). Proofreading is one activity that helps students to focus on the mechanics of writing and so can be used to reinforce grammatical skills. Or they might trade writing products with classmates in order to receive another perspective on the use of skills such as punctuation.

Finally, a caution is in order. It is important that students be provided with opportunities to write in which only the content—not mechanics—is the focus. In addition, expectations for what is important to a particular exercise should be explicit. For example, a math teacher might require that student-generated word problems include complete sentences and correct math terminology, while attention to spelling might be considered less important.

Chapter Four

Strategies for Writing to Learn

The primary goal for middle and high school teachers is to help students understand content-area material. However, what do teachers mean when they say they want their students to understand? Often, students can do multiplication problems without really understanding the process or why a particular answer is obtained. Similarly, students can recite historical facts without comprehending the significance of the events or the events leading up to or following an occurrence.

Jacobs talks about the importance of developing a more complex level of learning and states that "understanding is a problem-solving process that involves making meaning of content" (2002, 58). She explains, "Teaching for understanding, in part, involves choosing topics into which students can find their own points of entry; directly telling students the goals for their understanding; and developing assessments that allow students to demonstrate their understanding" (58).

"Writing is how students connect the dots in their knowledge" (National Commission on Writing in America's Schools and Colleges 2003, 3).

Writing to learn at the middle and secondary school levels provides a means through which students can both develop and demonstrate understanding. Through the use of writing activities, teachers engage their students in learning. As Sorenson explains:

> proponents of writing across the curriculum are quick to clarify that writing to learn is not the same as learning to write; but as flip sides of a single coin, the two support one another…. When content area teachers incorporate writing in all areas of the curriculum—social

studies, math, science, vocational education, business, foreign language, music, art, physical education, and language arts—students benefit in three ways: they have a resource for better understanding content; they practice a technique which aids retention; and they begin to write better (1991, online).

Writing to learn deepens student understanding by extending students' thinking. Like reading to learn, it is a meaning-making process that encourages students to organize their thoughts by labeling, objectifying, modifying, and building on concepts. It also engages learners by investing them in their own ideas and learning (Jacobs 2002).

In addition, Cochran suggests that opportunities for writing can help students develop the following skills:

- determining the relevance of information;
- distinguishing between fact and opinion;
- making a reasoned judgment;
- identifying unstated assumptions;
- detecting bias;
- detecting emotional language or appeal;
- identifying propaganda techniques;
- labeling value orientations and ideologies;
- judging authenticity of the author;
- recognizing adequacy of data;
- identifying the reasonableness of alternatives and solutions;
- predicting possible consequences; and
- testing conclusions or hypotheses (1993, 156-57).

Gunning addresses content-area teachers: "[Your] responsibility is two-fold: to teach skills unique to the subject matter and to teach students how to use reading and writing to learn subject matter content" (2003, 3).

In planning to incorporate opportunities for writing into their everyday instruction, teachers should remember that writing activities will be less successful if they are incorporated into the curriculum sporadically. Mitchell offers these suggestions for making writing a successful part of classroom instruction:

- show students you value it as part of the class;

- provide audiences for the writing (other students, other classes);

- keep content at the center of the writing process and look at what the writing says;

- realize writing is an act of trust on the part of students and that they must feel safe about sharing their writing;

- design writing activities that stretch students' knowledge and ask students to structure and synthesize what they know, not merely regurgitate what they are told; and

- give students choices about the form of the writing assignment whenever possible (1996, 97).

Several methods of incorporating writing-to-learn activities into content-area instruction are presented in this chapter. As you read them, reflect on the following questions posed by Jacobs:

> What strategies do you use to engage students in the process of making their own meaning? What strategies do you use to prepare and guide students in problem-solving—allowing students to integrate the "given" of what they bring to a text and the "new" that the text provides? What means do you provide for students to test assertions of their understanding before they have to demonstrate their understanding? How explicitly do you share with students the purposes of any given activity in light of your instructional goals? And how faithfully do the reading and writing strategies that you use serve your goals (2002, 61)?

Writing as a Pre-Reading Activity

Research supports the importance of advance organizers—in essence, a "mental road map" (Walberg and Paik 2004, 31)—in helping students process information presented through lecture and text. Use of pre-reading writing activities designed to increase student engagement with reading material by activating what students already know about a topic provides such a road map.

For example, in individual or group brainstorming sessions, students might make associations with the concepts they will read about and then write these down to use in a wrap-up exercise that checks predictions against the actual content. As an alternative, students could write down their personal thoughts or experiences relating to the topic. Autobiographical writing before reading increases understanding of a text, engagement in discussion, and understanding of characters; also, students who write before reading stories tend to like the stories better (White 1992, 1995). This technique easily could be used in any content-area classroom. For example, when beginning the study of geometry, a teacher could ask his/her students to write down some things they already know about shapes.

Previewing Texts

This strategy encourages students to preview texts and to record their pre-reading ideas. As students read, they refer to these notes adding, refining, and revising their understanding in light of the text.

Teachers wishing to implement this strategy in their classrooms should pose an open-ended question related to the topic of the reading before students read the text. They then should encourage students to consider their prior information related to the question and/or topic and to record their responses to the opening question—perhaps in journals that they routinely use for the class. Once this has been done, students can gather in small groups to share their responses. Students should be encouraged to look for similarities or differences in their ideas, to summarize these, and to generate additional ideas and questions. After 15-20 minutes, bring students back to a large group and record their ideas on chart paper. Finally, have students read the text, using their journals and the classroom discussion as a guide.

Previewing also can be adapted as a post-reading strategy in which students discuss a reading, explore their understandings and interpretations of the reading, and develop initial written responses.

Free Writes

Similar to some prewriting techniques already discussed, "free writes" is a term loosely describing informal writing opportunities that encourage students to focus on content with little to no expectation that the product will be "graded" from the perspective of mechanics. In addition, most free-write assignments are typically expected to take only a short period of time.

While free-write exercises can be used in a variety of ways in a classroom, they can be particularly useful in helping students develop their own "road maps" before reading or teacher presentations. In addition, research points to other potential benefits of providing students with free-write opportunities; for example:

- Free writing increases comfort and decreases the self-consciousness many students associate with writing (Veit 1981).

- Free writing makes it clear that writing is a process, not a final product (Veit 1981).

- Free writing, especially in conjunction with a prewriting prompt, helps students move from writing at the sentence level to writing at the text level (Knudson 1989).

- Free writing and writing feedback focused on meaning and ideas rather than error correction improves students' overall writing quality (Song 1998).

- Free writing that includes talking and discussion as part of the process creates the kind of communication-rich environment that fosters experimentation and confidence (Reid 1983).

- Free writing about particular texts increases reading comprehension (Williams 1992).

Merritt describes use of a particular free-write exercise—time-lapse writings—that can be used before a topic is introduced and then again at other points during the unit:

> The teacher collects these free writes and gives them back to students at the end of the unit for reflection. Students then write a final five-minute paragraph describing the progression of their thinking about the topic as the unit progressed (2003, 18).

Admit/Exit Slips

The Admit/Exit Slips strategy includes both pre- and post-reading elements, with the admit slips intended to activate student's prior knowledge and the exit slips to provide closure to a classroom discussion. To prepare students for classroom discussion, students are given an index card on arrival at the classroom and asked to respond to a question such as "What was the most important point in your assigned reading?" or "What questions do you have about the assignment?" or "What aspects of today's lesson are you most interested in discussing?" (Andrews 1997, 141). Completion of an admit slip serves as a "ticket" into the classroom, and discussion of students' answers provides the basis for initial classroom conversation. Andrews elaborates on another benefit of this strategy: "The slips also provide a nice model of activating students' schema and allow the class to have a voice in the direction of the day's lesson" (141).

The use of exit slips provides closure to classroom discussions and a means of summarizing what has been said. At the end of a class period, students are again provided with an index card and asked to reflect on the day's lesson and respond to a question such as "What did you learn today?" or "What is still confusing to you?" (Andrews 1997, 141). In addition to providing a tool to help students mentally organize the material that was presented, information gleaned from students' responses can be used to plan the following day's agenda.

Journal Writing

Although the use of journals began in language arts classes, they are being used in an increasing number of other content-area classes. Teachers who use journal writing should keep two key elements in mind. First, journal writing should serve a specific instructional purpose. Second, the exercise should be designed to demonstrate to students that it is not just "busy work." By explicitly explaining the purpose to students and then using what is written—for example, as a communication tool or to help students review key concepts presented in class—teachers ensure students begin to understand that journal writing can be a valuable tool for their learning.

Journals can be used for a variety of purposes in the middle and high school classroom, including to:

- record experiences;
- stimulate interest in a topic;
- explore thinking;
- personalize learning;

- develop interpretations;

- wonder, predict, and hypothesize;

- engage the imagination;

- ask questions;

- activate prior knowledge;

- assume the role of another person; and

- share experiences with trusted readers (Tompkins 1998, 222, 224).

For example, Ameig talks about use of student journaling in middle school music classes. Students "respond to questions regarding specific examples of music and are expected to share their responses" (1993, 30). Students then use their journals during other activities that reinforce learning; for example:

> Having relays in which teams review their journals to answer questions drawn from a hat can help students prepare for tests.... Of course, the best part is that in their eagerness to play the game, they forget that they are learning (32).

Students should write in their journals on a regular schedule and preferably on a daily basis. At Canajoharie Middle School in Canajoharie, N.Y., Donnalee Bowerman begins class each day with a journal-writing activity. As she explains, "It gives my students, who have great difficulty with written language, one time when spelling, punctuation, and grammar don't count.... This lets them express themselves in writing without the pressure they typically have when doing assignments. It ensures they have one positive writing experience each day" (Hopkins 1999, online).

Some teachers ask their students to keep personal journals for the duration of the school year, while others alternate the type of journal used based on the social studies or science theme cycle or the literature focus unit being studied. When a new type of journal is introduced, teachers should explain the purpose of the assigned journal writing activity, how to gather ideas, model writing an entry, and explain how (or if) entries will be shared with the class. Students can write independently once they understand the type of entry they are assigned to write.

Journal writing often provides a "safe space" for student writing. Teachers who feel a need to hold their students accountable for their journal writing

Five Suggestions for Ensuring Effective Use of Journals in the Classroom

1) *Modeling*. The best way to help students learn how to engage in thoughtful journal writing is to keep one yourself. Write about your experiences as a teacher, reader, parent, cook, golfer. Show students model entries from your journal. Talk about how you go about the process of keeping a journal. Think aloud to show them your thinking process in creating an entry.

2) *Criteria*. Students should regularly select a journal entry as the basis for more formal written work. In making a selection and working to expand and revise it, students need to be able to evaluate their own work according to clear criteria (e.g., Is it organized in a way that makes sense to the reader? Does it use the academic vocabulary of the subject area?) Criteria can be provided to students or developed with students through modeling and analyzing samples.

3) *Feedback*. Far more important than grading is feedback. Give students a grade, and that's the end of the process; there is little reason or encouragement to expand, refine, or explore further. But give them constructive, criteria-based suggestions on how they might improve, or provoke them to deepen their thinking through questions, and a different dynamic emerges—one that's in keeping with the cyclical nature of the writing process. For this reason, students should receive at least one or two personal responses to their writing every other week.

4) *Blending choice and assigned entries*. Good classroom writing does not begin with statements like this: "Write about whatever you want." Instead, you should strive to develop a structure that encourages controlled freedom. Controlled freedom means that the students are not constrained by overly specific assignments (e.g., What powers does the executive branch hold?) but that the freedom students have to explore ideas is tied to essential learning and themes. By blending provocative, open-ended journal assignments (e.g., Why do you think people claim that Shakespeare is the ultimate universal writer?) with choice-based question menus that provide students with options about how best to respond, you can create a perfect balance between freedom and focus.

5) *Samples*. Experts in all disciplines use journals. Bring in samples of journal writing from masters like Picasso, Thoreau, Darwin, Poincare, and Churchill. Ask students to discover and discuss what makes for great journal writing (Strong et al. 2002, 136-37).

can do so by noting the completeness and appropriateness of student entries, but should not take grammar, spelling, or other language mechanics into account (Ross 1998).

Ross talks about the concern that teachers may have regarding the time requirement needed by teachers who ask students to write in journals:

> What you should keep in mind . . . is that journals are only as much work as you want them to be. It is you, the teacher, who decides how many entries you require and how long the entries must be. You determine whether you will comment on each entry, on random entries, or just on the entries the students have marked as ones they particularly want you to read. You also decide how extensive your

---

Prompts for Journal Writing

- If I could give one piece of advice to the colonists, that advice would be . . .

- Describe a dream you had recently. Provide as many details as possible.

- The best lesson my grandparent (or any relative or adult) ever taught me was . . .

- If I could travel to the moon, this is a description of what I would see.

- If I lived in a rain forest, I would . . .

- In 20 years, I will be . . .

- Tell about an event in your life that has caused a change in you.

- If I had $100, I would . . .

- My worst mistake was . . .

- Your school needs to hold a fund-raiser for the basketball team. Propose three fund-raising options and explain why you would choose each, and the logistics of each event.

- You have the freedom to travel to any city or country in the world. Where would you go and why?

- What would you do if you were president of the United States?

---

comments will be. In other words, you set the rules for journals. The one clear imperative, in my mind, is that you do read your students' journals. If you don't, students won't take their journal writing seriously, and you won't learn anything about how your students are progressing or what questions they have about the class work (1998, 189).

Dialogue Journals

A dialogue journal is an informal, written conversation between a student and another person (usually a teacher, but it could also be a peer or parent), in which participants chat, either about issues of importance to them or about material they are reading. Benefits of using dialogue journals include:

- Students have an opportunity to write for a genuine audience.

- Teachers have one-on-one time with students that otherwise might not be feasible.

- Dialogue in these journals has the potential to go beyond the parameters of usual classroom discourse because the conversation is more private, and those who are shy or unsure about the value of their own ideas may express themselves more readily.

The benefits of dialogue journals are underscored by a case study of two veteran English teachers who introduced them in their classrooms (Gross 1992). Both teachers found the students enjoyed this activity, were more engaged in reading, and liked sharing ideas with peers. Dialogue journals are an effective way to get students involved with information being presented, because the goal of such journals is not to write polished essays, but typically to help students to become more aware of content without having to worry about elements such as grammar and punctuation.

Guidelines for students who write in reading dialogue journals might include:

- Express your personal responses to reading—your opinions, feelings, likes, and dislikes.

- Relate the material you read to your own experiences or information you have learned before.

- Don't worry about spelling and grammar. Expressing your thoughts is more important.

- Talk about things you don't understand, or ask questions about what is happening or why something is happening.

- Make predictions about what will happen or what other information will be presented in the rest of the chapter or book. As you continue reading, keep track of which predictions come true, but don't worry about being wrong.

- Give specific reasons why you feel the book is helpful or interesting (or not), such as the writing style or subject matter (Fuhler 1994; Wells 1993).

Because teachers are flexible about grammar and other language rules when reading the dialogue journals, those students who are not native English speakers may feel more free to write than they might when given other writing assignments. Students speaking very little English could even draw pictures to express their ideas, to which teachers might respond initially with pictures and a few words. Dialogue journals also can provide opportunities for exchanging cultural knowledge between people of different backgrounds.

Journals may be used as a forum for discussing articles or books students have chosen within an independent reading program. Conversations can be recorded in a notebook (preferably a spiral bound one, in order to resist wear and tear). At the back of the notebook, students can keep a log of what they have read and when they completed a reading. This serves as an easy reference for teachers, students, and parents.

Students should write regularly in dialogue journals—ideally at least once a week. Because dialogue journals require regular reading and responding from teachers, time management is an important concern. Keep in mind, however, dialogue journals are not simply an added demand on the teaching load—at times, they can replace some kinds of written work. A middle school teacher recalls:

I remember suffering through piles of junior high book reports, the dullest writing I've ever read. By contrast, the [kids'] letters are a constant source of surprise, pleasure, and stimulation. And what they replaced—book reports, worksheets, quizzes, and tests—ate up more time than keeping up with my correspondents ever will (Atwell 1998, 198).

Students should have the opportunity to write to diverse audiences, such as peers and parents. It has been found that students write different kinds of journal entries to peers than to teachers; for example, students are more likely to recommend books to one another than to teachers (Wells 1993), and they write more often about their emotional reactions to a book when writing to a peer (Atwell 1998). In addition, involving parents in the dialogue journal process is a powerful way to link home and school (Fuhler 1994).

Reciprocal Teaching Journals

Reciprocal teaching journals help build students' summarizing skills by applying the steps of reciprocal teaching—asking questions, managing new vocabulary, predicting, and summarizing—to a journal format. Students process new knowledge better when they have the opportunity to think through it, pose questions, and summarize ideas in their own words. Reciprocal teaching journals provide students with a writing tool for engaging in these practices.

Jones describes a suggested approach for implementing reciprocal teaching journals:

1) Put students in groups of four.

2) Distribute one notecard to each member of the group identifying each person's unique role.

   - summarizer

   - questioner

   - clarifier

   - predictor

3) Have students read a few paragraphs of the assigned text selection. Encourage them to use note-taking strategies such as selective underlining or sticky-notes to help them better prepare for their role in the discussion.

4) At the given stopping point, the Summarizer will highlight the key ideas up to this point in the reading.

5) The Questioner will then pose questions about the selection:

- unclear parts

- puzzling information

- connections to other concepts already learned

- motivations of the agents or actors or characters

- etc.

6) The Clarifier will address confusing parts and attempt to answer the questions that were just posed.

7) The Predictor can offer guesses about what the author will tell the group next or, if it's a literary selection, the predictor might suggest what the next events in the story will be.

8) The roles in the group then switch one person to the right, and the next selection is read. Students repeat the process using their new roles. This continues until the entire selection is read (2001, online).

Learning Logs

Learning logs are typically seen as more structured than most journals and are similar to a laboratory notebook that is sometimes assigned in science classes. WAC Clearinghouse describes an approach to using learning logs that could be used in any content-area class:

Students write for about five minutes, often summarizing class lecture material, noting the key points of a lab session, or raising unanswered questions from a preceding class. Sometimes, students write for just one or two minutes both at the beginning and end of a class session. At the beginning, they might summarize the key points from the preceding class (so that the teacher doesn't have to remind them about the previous day's class). At the end of class students might write briefly about a question such as:

- What one idea that we talked about today most interested you and why?

- What was the clearest point we made today?

Writing to Learn Activities: Some Examples

Reading Journals: Students use the left half of the page or the left sheet of an opened notebook for recording what the reading is about. Teachers can ask for quite a lot of detail in this half of the reading journal so that students get practice in summarizing entire articles or summarizing particular arguments, identifying main ideas, noting key details, and choosing pertinent quotations, among other crucial reading skills. On the right half of the page, students jot down any questions they have or any connections they can make between readings or between readings and class discussions. At the beginning of the semester, the right half of the journal is dotted with questions, most of which can be answered quickly at the beginning of a discussion session in class. By the end of the semester, students will sometimes fill two right-hand columns for every reading. At this point, the questions are far richer (rarely about content) and the connections point out that students are integrating the readings and class work on their own.

Generic and Focused Summaries: Depending on the level of detail that might be useful for each assignment, have students write out a paragraph or a page of summary for each assigned reading. When collected in a reading journal or learning log, these summaries help students understand readings more fully when they are first assigned and remember them clearly for later tests or synthesis assignments. You might also consider asking students to do more focused summaries. By providing key questions about the reading, you can help students narrow in on the main ideas you want them to emphasize and remember from a reading.

Annotations: Unlike the summary that attempts a listing of the key points in a reading, an annotation typically asks students to note key ideas and briefly evaluate strengths and weaknesses in an article. Annotations often ask students to note the purpose and scope of a reading and to relate the reading to a particular course project. Have students annotate (and eventually compare) readings assigned for the class, or ask students to compile annotations to supplement the course readings. Each student's annotations can be distributed to the class in one handout or through electronic media (Web forum, email).

Response Papers: Unlike a summary, the response paper specifically asks students to react to assigned readings. Students might write responses that analyze specified features of a reading (the quality of data, the focus of research reported, the validity of research design, the effectiveness of logical argument). Or they might write counter-arguments. To extend these response papers (which can be any length the instructor sets), consider combining them into another assignment—a position paper or a research-based writing assignment.

Synthesis Papers: The synthesis paper asks students to work with several readings and to draw commonalities out of those readings. Particularly when individual readings over-simplify a topic, the synthesis paper helps students grapple with the complexity of issues and ideas. Like other writing-to-learn tasks, the synthesis paper can be shorter and less formal, or assigned at or near the end of a sequence leading to a more formal paper.

Focusing a Discussion: When a discussion seems to be taking off in several directions, dominated by just a few students, or emotionally charged, stop the discussion and ask students to write either what they saw as the main threads of the discussion or where the discussion might most profitably go. After writing for a few minutes, students will often be better able to identify and stay on productive tracks of discussion. Or, after asking a few students to read their writing aloud, the teacher can decide how best to redirect the discussion.

Analyzing the Process: Sometimes students are baffled by the explanations teachers give of how things happen because teachers move too quickly or easily through the process analysis. A quick run-through of an equation is often just not enough for students struggling to learn new material. A more useful approach to process analysis—from the learners' point of view—is to trace *in writing* the steps required to complete the process or to capture the thinking that leads from one step to the next. Students can either write while or after they complete each problem. Particularly when students get stuck in the middle of a problem, writing down why they completed the steps they did will usually help someone else (a classmate, tutor, or teacher) see why the student experienced a glitch in problem-solving. Similarly, teachers can look over the process analyses to see if students have misapplied fundamental principles or if they are making simple mistakes. In effect, students can concentrate on problem-solving rather than on minor details, and they can move from simple procedures followed by rote into a deeper understanding of why they are solving problems appropriately.

The Problem Statement: Teachers usually set up the problems and ask students to provide solutions. Two alternatives to this standard procedure will give students practice with both framing *and* solving problems:

- After you introduce a new concept, ask students to write out a theoretical or practical problem that the concept might help to solve. Students can exchange these problems and write out solutions, thus ensuring that they understand the concept clearly and fully.

- Ask students to write out problem statements before they come to class. Students are likely to frame such a problem more concretely than they might otherwise do in preparing for a conference, and the resulting discussion is likely to be more productive.

Another version of this exercise is to have students write a problem statement that is passed on to another student whose job it is to answer it. Such peer answers are especially useful in large classes (excerpted from WAC Clearinghouse, Colorado State University n.d., online).

- What was the foggiest point?

- What do you still not understand about the concept we've been discussing?

- If you had to restate the concept in your own terms, how would you do that?

- How does today's discussion build on yesterday's?

Such questions can provide continuity from class to class, but they can also give teachers a quick glimpse into how well the class materials are getting across. Some teachers pick up the complete learning logs every other week to skim through them, and others pick up a single response, particularly after introducing a key concept. These occasional snapshots of students' comprehension help teachers quickly gauge just how well students understand the material. Teachers can then tailor the following class to meet students' needs (n.d., online).

Reflective Writing

Strong et al. promote reflective writing as a strategy to engage learners in text, since opportunities for reflective writing can encourage students to "write about their growing understanding of the content of the reading and of their own reading process" (2002, 149). Reflective writing also promotes metacognitive thinking, which research has linked to increased student motivation and achievement. On this point, Strong et al. assert that "when students are asked to think about their own thinking, they learn to be more self-regulated in their learning and begin to see what kinds of thinking come naturally to them and what kinds pose difficulties. By using writing to record this metacognition, students overtly expose their thinking processes as they read" (2002, 149).

Teachers who wish to engage their students in reflective writing activities should first provide students with a reading on a given topic, then ask them to stop after they have read the first two or three key ideas in the reading. At this point, students should be asked to consider several reflective questions. They should organize their thoughts on these questions and record their responses. Students can finish reading the passage and then form small groups to share and compare their thoughts. A concluding activity should be

Learning Log Responses to Reading:
Suggested Prompts

Provide students with one of these prompts after modifying it to address your instructional objectives. Or allow them to choose from among a few of them. Write about:

- Any passage or item that puzzles you

- Any passage or item that intrigues you

- Three (two, one) things you disagree with

- Three (two, one) new concepts and your definitions of them

- How this reading relates to _____ (your life, what we've been studying, etc.)

- Two things this reading has in common with _____

- What you think it would be like to live in _____

- Your reaction to _____

- Three things you think are important enough to discuss in class

- A cause/effect flow chart

- How you can use this knowledge in your own life

- Something the reading reminds you of

- What you think it means and why you think that

- Why _____ is important

- How the writer of this passage makes it easy or difficult to understand (University of Texas Center for Reading & Language Arts 2003, online).

developed to encourage students to summarize their thoughts and develop their own reflective questions—both metacognitive skills.

A teacher who uses this strategy explains it to her students in this way:

> As you examine what you've written and your reflections, read your
> writing slowly, paying attention to your own inner voice. In your

groups, I want you to pool your answers to the questions into a brief summary of what you've read so far, noting what you found difficult and why. Your journal writing and summarizing will give you a sense of what some technical writers go through as they write. Understanding the process of writing can sometimes make it easier to read what others have written (Strong et al. 2002, 149).

Integrating Writing and Cooperative Learning

Although both journal writing and reflective writing as described above would typically be described as practices involving introspection, other strategies build on more collaborative models. One of these is Think-Pair-Share. It is not uncommon for students sometimes to have difficulty uncovering the meaning of a text. By working collaboratively, however, students may be better able to identify the "big ideas" and to further their understanding of a text. This understanding can then be used as the basis of a free write on the topic.

The Think-Pair-Share strategy first requires students to read a text and write down what they believe are the four main ideas of the text. Next, students pair up to share their ideas and to select the two most important ideas from their lists. Then, each student pair joins another student pair, and the group of four shares its two ideas and reaches an agreement on the single most important idea. After this, students free write for five minutes on the selected idea, explaining what they know about it. When the free write is complete, students return to their groups of four and share their writing. Finally, students can convene as a large group and share their "big ideas" and free writes. If desired, teachers may want to allow students to expand on their free write by further developing their ideas at some point during the unit or lesson.

Merritt describes another approach—which she calls snapshot summaries— for helping students mentally synthesize the information generated during a collaborative learning exercise:

> After students work collaboratively on an activity, they individually write a five-minute snapshot summary of the content of the discussion, activity, problem-solving opportunity, or experiment that they just experienced. They then regroup briefly to compare "snapshots" and add to or correct their snapshots as necessary to provide a record of details for later review (2003, 18).

Teacher Andrea del Rio follows free writing in her high school geometry class-room with whole-class collaborative activity that she believes helps her students to make sense of how geometry concepts build on one another. She writes:

> It's always instructive to hear them negotiating their ideas. You really get a chance to see how their minds work—how they interact, think, and express themselves. After they're done negotiating, we talk about each group's ideas, focusing on how they justified their decision and looking for both the connections and disparities between different groups' ideas. Then, we reach our final consensus. As a class, we decide which group's idea best captures the essential message of the text, and once they have that, they use it as the conceptual foundation for their free writing.
>
> After this is all done—the negotiation of ideas, the free writing, the reading aloud—students have a great foundation for future learning (Strong et al. 2002, 145).

Other Strategies for Using Writing to Promote Learning

Klingner and Vaughn describe a strategy they term "getting the gist"—"identifying the most important idea in a section of text" (1998, 34):

> The goal of getting the gist is to teach students to restate in their own words the most important point as a way of making sure they have understood what they have read. This strategy can improve students' understanding and memory of what they have learned.... Carmel Johnson taught the gist this way. She would ask students to think about the passage they had just read and to write down the most important person, place, or thing in the sentence. She would then call on individual students to obtain their responses. She would ask other students which answer was best and why. Then she would ask students to work alone or in pairs to write the gist of the passage. She would then ask students to read their gists aloud and to invite other students to comment on the effectiveness of the gists, thus refining the skills of all students (34).

Mitchell suggests the use of "what if...?" writing exercises that "tap into higher level thinking skills . . . to figure out how the absence of something would have an impact on something else" (1996, 94). She provides examples that could be used in a variety of content areas; for example:

Writing To Learn Activities: Additional Examples

Anticipation Guides: Statements such as the following tend to promote thinking and discussion: "All people are born basically good," "Science gives us definite answers to the questions we ask," "Math requires creativity," "The Internet has improved life for everyone," or "Art is only effective when it causes controversy." More specific statements can be designed for any type of unit. The student indicates that he or she either agrees or disagrees with the statement. Next, the student can be asked to write a brief paragraph about the statement that he/she feels the most strongly about. Students then discuss the statements in small groups or as a class.

Crossword Puzzles: Individually or in pairs students generate crossword puzzles using a list of terms related to a unit of study. Then, they can swap puzzles with other students as a way of reviewing content. The students focus not only on the terms themselves but also on writing the clues in their own words. Puzzles can be created online at www.puzzlemaker.com.

Hot Cards: Students are given a note card and instructed to respond to a prompt. If the teacher wants to check for understanding, he or she can instruct students to write three quick sentences summarizing what they learned in class that day, list 10 facts about a topic, write five quiz questions they would like to be asked about the day's lesson, or give a quick explanation of their understanding of a concept. If the teacher wants to find out where students are having difficulties, he or she can instruct students to list any questions they have about the topic, tell about something they don't understand right now, or describe something that confuses them. The teacher can either check the cards after class or can use a few minutes of class time to address questions/comments on the cards with the class. The benefit of using note cards rather than paper is that they can be easily sorted, they limit the amount of information the student needs to provide, and they can be easily stored for later use.

Venn Diagrams: Students are given two or more concepts and are told to draw interlocking circles that overlap in some places but are separate in others. They then write in what they know about each concept. They show their understanding of each concept's relationship to other concepts by writing information that is "shared" by concepts in the part of the circles that overlap and the information that is distinct to each concept in the outer part of the circle.

Telegrams: Students are instructed to write a telegram summarizing the day's lesson or their understanding of a concept. Because telegrams make an economical use of language, students must choose their words carefully to be concise yet get across meaning.

Brainstorming: Students can be instructed to brainstorm by making lists, by webbing (put a concept in a circle in the middle of a page and "web" out associations with that concept), or creating concept maps. Teachers can use brainstorming activities at the beginning of a unit to help students gather prior knowledge about a topic, during the drafting stage of writing if a student gets stuck and needs more ideas, or as a prewriting activity during topic generation.

Bumper Stickers: To help students elicit the essence of a historical period, scientific discovery, health danger, artistic technique, or technological concept, students can be instructed to create a bumper sticker advertising or taking a position on the concept being studied. Students should be reminded that bumper stickers are short and capture the essence of something in a memorable way.

Lecture Interruption: Interrupt a lecture at a surprising moment with a five-minute quickwrite. Students can be instructed to make a quick list of information they remember from the lecture so far (without looking at their notes) or review their notes to list higher-level questions or just questions borne of curiosity that might be raised about the information presented so far.

Couplets: Students create couplets (two rhyming lines with a regular rhythm) about terms such as "macroeconomics," "behaviorism," or "topology" to help them remember the meaning of the term as well as distinguish the term from others (such as microeconomics, behavior, or topography). For example, astronomy helps us understand the stars; astrology helps us know what fate is ours.

Metaphors: Students can generate metaphors (surprising comparisons between things that are not usually thought of as similar) to help illustrate their understanding of a concept, historical event, musical style, or technological innovation. For example, they can create a metaphor for items such as a state lottery, jazz, graph, e-commerce, Victorian Age, pollution, physiology, or New Criticism. For example, the heart is the engine of the body, pumping blood to keep the machine running.

Want Ads: Students can create want ads to show their understanding of literary characters or historical figures by composing want ads that depict something the person seeks, wants to sell, or could offer as a service (excerpted from Merritt 2003, 16-18).

Writing to Learn Activities: Additional Examples

Solving Real Problems: Ask individuals or groups to analyze a real problem—gleaned from industry reports, scientific journals, personal experience, management practices, law, etc. Students must write about the problem and a solution they could implement.

Pre-Test Warm-Ups: Ask students to generate problems for an upcoming test. Students might work collaboratively either to generate problems or to draft solutions. By asking each student or group of students to generate problems, students will cover the course material more fully than they might otherwise do in studying. Moreover, if you assure students that at least some of the test material will draw on the problems students generate, they are more likely to take both the problems and solutions more seriously. Furthermore, if students don't understand the material, they will surely find out as they write questions for the exams!

What Counts as a Fact?: Select two or more treatments of the same issue, problem, or research. For example, you might bring in an article on a new diet drug from *USA Today, The Wall Street Journal,* and the *Journal of Dietetics.* Ask students to write about what constitutes proof or facts in each article and explain why the articles draw on different kinds of evidence, as well as the amount of evidence that supports stated conclusions. Alternatively, ask students to look at a range of publications within a discipline—trade journals, press releases, scientific reports, first-person narratives, and so on. Have them ask the same kinds of questions about evidence and the range of choices writers make as they develop and support arguments in your field.

The Believing Game and the Doubting Game: This writing activity simply calls for students to write briefly:

- first, in support of an idea, concept, methodology, thesis;

- second, in opposition to it.

As students complete this writing activity based on a course reading or controversy in the field, they become more adept at understanding the complexity of issues and arguments.

(Excerpted from WAC Clearinghouse, Colorado State University n.d., online).

- What if the setting in this story changed?

- What if we had no moon?

- What if your heart had only three chambers instead of four?

- What if there were no fractional parts in real life?

- What if there were no black or white pigment? How would it affect your painting?

- What if people didn't sweat during and after exercise?

- What if spark plugs didn't exist?

- What would music sound like if there were no major modes? (94).

In Summary

As evidenced by the nature of the activities described in this chapter, "writing to learn requires the teacher to change from being the source of information to being a guide who assists students [in finding] their own knowledge" (Johnson et al. 1993, 157). Each of the strategies discussed encourages students to demonstrate their understanding of course content and to reflect on their own understandings (Andrews 1997).

Teachers who have implemented these or similar approaches cite the following benefits:

- Students become more involved in the workings of the class because the writing motivates them.

- Students learn what they know and what they have questions about and become more aware of their own learning as they write about it.

- Students demonstrate higher-level thinking skills elicited by the writing.

- Teachers can assess what the class understands and doesn't understand through student writing (Mitchell 1996, 96-7).

Johnson et al. aptly describe writing to learn as a process emphasizing "better thinking" (1993, 155). As one teacher explained, "[Writing to learn activities have] made me not such a structured teacher anymore. [They have] made me better able to let the students do the learning.... I am a learner also, with the students" (Johnson et al. 1993, 158).

Chapter Five

Writing in Mathematics, Science, and Social Studies

While the previous chapter provided ideas for integrating writing opportunities across the curriculum, teachers within specific content areas understandably may be interested in how teachers in their discipline have used writing to promote student learning.

This chapter provides examples of how writing instruction and the teaching of the necessary related skills can be incorporated meaningfully into mathematics, science, and social studies classes.

Using Writing in Mathematics Classes

In response to the new interest in writing as a teaching technique, teachers of mathematics are beginning to incorporate writing activities into their daily instruction. The National Council of Teachers of Mathematics' *Standards for Mathematics Instruction* supports this integration: "Students should be encouraged to increase their ability to express themselves clearly and coherently…. The ability to write about mathematics should be particularly nurtured across the grades" (2000, online).

Countryman cites the importance of having students understand mathematics concepts—not just operations—and the way in which writing can support that. She writes, "To learn mathematics, students must construct it for themselves. They can only do that by exploring, justifying, representing, discussing, using, describing, investigating, predicting, in short by being active in the world. Writing is an ideal activity for such processes" (in Kroll and Halaby 1997, 55). Burns elaborates further, referring to writing in mathematics classes as "a window into what [students] understand, how they approach ideas, what misconceptions they harbor, and how they feel about what they're discovering" (1995, 40).

Four Ways to Have Students Write in Math Class

1. **Writing in journals or logs.**

2. **Writing the solutions to math problems.**

3. **Writing math essays.**

4. **Writing about learning (Burns 1995, 43).**

Kenyon explains that "writing down the thoughts and procedures involved for each of the steps of a problem solution adds yet another dimension to the processing. The problem solver can now clearly 'see' the steps of the solution described in written words and has immediate feedback for review and reflection. Writing encourages evaluation and modification for each of the steps" (in Kroll and Halaby 1997, 55).

To assist students in explaining their mathematical solutions, Strong et al. suggest following these five steps:

1) Assign students a word problem to solve in class. Students read the problem carefully and underline the question and the essential information.

2) Allow students to solve the problem. When they are finished, they should reflect on the process and list, in order, the steps they followed.

3) Work with students to use transitional words (e.g., first, next, then, finally) to convert steps into paragraph form.

4) Have students reread their explanations and ask: Does it include all the steps? Do any terms need clarification? Are the steps in the correct order? Are the transitional words well chosen?

5) Encourage students to revise and refine their explanations as necessary (2002, 149-50).

The use of journals in mathematics classes also is increasing. Bagley and Gallenberger see this as a positive trend because, in their view, journal writing in mathematics classes allows students to:

- participate by communicating ideas, questions, or suggestions when they are too shy or intimidated to do so in front of the entire class;

- write freely without concern about spelling, punctuation, style, and so on;

- summarize, organize, relate, and associate ideas;

- define, discuss, or describe an idea or concept;

- experiment with, create, or discover mathematics independently;

- review topics;

- reflect on topics by summarizing goals, strategies, reactions, accomplishments, or frustrations; and

- openly express positive and negative feelings and frustrations (1992, 661).

By writing in a journal, students are forced to examine their ideas and reflect on their solutions. Writing helps students articulate their thoughts more clearly. Another benefit of this approach, asserts Halaby, is that the teacher is able to see the progression of students' mathematical thinking and problem-solving ability in their journals (Kroll and Halaby 1997). This allows teachers to adapt their instruction to students' needs. Says one teacher:

> I always read the journals and adapt my instruction for the next day based on what I read. I may have to revisit a topic to clarify something that was not understood. I make a note to revamp explanations for future classes. Sometimes I see that the students know more than I thought. The insights they demonstrate are helpful for altering my approach to topics (Goldsby and Cozza 2002, 519).

In addition to reflecting on or explaining solutions in journals, some teachers assign a specific mathematics-related writing assignment several times a week. Bagley and Gallenberger offer the following sample topics:

- Write a letter to a junior high school student. Explain to the youngster how to solve a quadratic equation (or any algebra skill) and the reasons that knowing this skill is important to an algebra student.

- Display a picture. Construct a word problem about the picture that can be solved mathematically. Share your problem with your partner and solve it.

- Write three questions that you believe would be good test questions. Be sure to include answers to your questions.

- List some of the common mistakes you have made in class, on homework, on tests, and so on.

- What is the most important idea you have learned in [class] this week?

- Write a paragraph containing as many of these words as possible:_____.

- Explain how you study for tests.

- What do you do best in mathematics class? (1992, 661-62).

Russek describes writing tasks assigned by teacher Donna Kelly in an introductory algebra course:

> She presents a "math trick" on Monday, and the students have to write why it works in a couple of paragraphs that are due on Friday. She requires complete, coherent sentences, and stresses that students check spelling and grammar. The assignment is graded mainly on content; however, she does take off points for incoherent, incomplete sentences and excessive spelling errors (1998, 37).

In her own class, Russek uses prompts such as: "Write a letter to a classmate who could not attend class today so that she/he will understand what we did and learn as much as you did. Be as complete as possible" (37). Other prompts she suggests include "Now I understand...," "I can help myself by doing...," and "You can help me by..." (42).

As another example, Kenyon (2000) suggests students be asked to write brief paragraphs comparing key concepts such as a line and a plane. These paragraphs are discussed, providing both review and an opportunity to clarify understanding.

Finally, Pugalee (1997) talks about the use of writing as a diagnostic tool for mathematics teachers—similar to the techniques previously discussed by Goldsby and Cozza. For example, students in an algebra class were asked to "explain in detail how the x- and y-intercepts can be found when graphing parabolas" (309). Students displayed a range of understanding of key concepts needed to solve the problems, and the student writing provided:

> . . . important information about the concepts that the student possesses. Such insights allow the teacher to give the proper instructions and explanations to clarify and correct the misconceptions (309).

Using Writing in Science Classes

The trend in science education is toward inquiry-based learning—an approach that requires students to think critically by asking questions, planning and conducting investigations using appropriate tools to answer their questions, and presenting their findings to others. Writing is an important element of this process, as students must record their findings and write their conclusions. It also is important to have students explain science concepts in their own words, as this shows their understanding of the concept and their ability to explain it in a way that is meaningful to them. Wittrock and Barrow write, "The important element in science writing is guiding children to express their learning in their own words . . . [and providing] ample time for students to share orally and revise their work after they hear others' ideas" (2000, 37).

Inquiry-based science requires students to write problems and solutions, to design investigations and describe how to solve problems, to compare and contrast alternate approaches, and possibly to describe how technology can be used to solve a problem. As students move through these processes, they will need to plan, compose, and evaluate their writing—all important skills in the writing process (Pugalee, DiBiase, and Wood 1999).

The National Science Resources Center suggests science and literacy skills may increase simultaneously because:

> Language is best learned in context . . . [and] a well-structured science curriculum can provide the needed context. Inquiry science also challenges students to ask questions and to look for answers. In many cases, that search for answers takes them to the Web, to the library, or even back to their science book. Wherever the search leads them, students end up reading in order to find answers. Students are challenged to think about and discuss their experiences. Writing— summarizing, synthesizing, or reflecting on what they've read—is the natural next step (2001, online).

Many teachers of science, after conducting an experiment or an investigation, may choose to have their students discuss their findings in groups before doing any writing. In some cases, conversations may center on explanations or scientific arguments; in others, students may discuss the process and why certain results were seen. Oftentimes, after some discussion has taken place, students will be asked to discuss their findings in writing, whether in the form of a lab report, journal entry, or essay (Strong et al. 2002).

Teacher Mario Godoy-Gonzalez refers to the thrill of scientific discovery as a "springboard for developing [students'] language skills" (Boss 2002, 17) and believes that writing "has been the key to unlocking students' understanding of science" (18). As an English as a Second Language teacher, Godoy-Gonzalez looks for ways to engage his students in both the subject matter and writing. After creating a rhyme based on students' responses to a question, he turned to poetry as a medium of expression. He says:

> For many of my students, writing an essay seems too hard. It takes so many words, many of which are technical. By the time they look up a scientific term in the dictionary, they have lost the sense of where they wanted to use the word in their writing. With poetry, however, students found their voice. Poetry gets the brain and the heart working together (Boss 2002, 18).

Godoy-Gonzalez took the exercise one step further and showed students the many forms poetry can take—haiku, acrostic, quatrain. Working in groups, students drafted poems together and helped each other revise and improve their writings. Soon, his students learned that "writing never ends" and that writers are "always involved in improving, revising, expanding" (Boss 2002, 18).

To assist students in learning to write within the sciences, teachers should provide students with models of writing, as Godoy-Gonzalez did when he created his initial rhyme in front of his students. Models can take many forms—earth science teacher Terrell Childs uses online scientific journals as models for his students (Strong et al. 2002). Other teachers may choose to keep a file of outstanding student examples that they share with their classes each year.

Using Writing in Social Studies Classes

Students often do as much writing during social studies lessons as they do during English or language arts classes. To help students improve their writing as they complete these assignments, teachers need to identify the specific social studies content and skills they want their students to learn by writing. In addition, teachers also must design assignments in which the level of difficulty of the task matches the level of the goal (e.g., simple recall questions if the goal is only for students to learn the information) (Brostoff 1979).

In recent years, state tests have begun asking students to read, interpret, and write about a group of texts sharing a common theme or concept. While this used to be common only on advanced placement tests in History and English, it is now becoming more common on standardized social studies tests at all levels, 6-12. Given this, teachers need to ensure their students are prepared for the kind of reading that will make thoughtful writing possible (Strong et al. 2002).

Strong et al. provide this five-step process for teachers to model for their students to help them succeed in writing these essays:

1) *Analyze the question or test item for key words and topics.* For example, one test gives students three texts: In the first, a Chinese student describes her first three months in an American school, the second describes a classroom during an air raid drill, and the last is a poem on teaching. Students are asked to discuss how these three texts contribute to their understanding of how teachers help students learn. Thus, the key topic is how teachers help students learn.

2) *Generate what is already known about the topic.* Once students have determined the central topic, they should create a concept map that contains everything they know about the topic.

3) *Use this prior knowledge to actively search for examples in the text.* With prior knowledge out in the open and organized, reading becomes focused and active. Students should annotate the texts as they read them, using underlining, arrows, margin notes, and the like to mark and contextualize the important information.

4) *Move text annotations into the concept map.* At this point, students should expand and revise their concept maps by putting the information from the texts into their original concept maps. This way, students have comprehensive maps that include their own ideas and the examples and ideas from the texts—exactly what they need in order to discuss how the texts contribute to their understanding of how teachers help students learn.

5) *Lay out the sequence for writing.* Thinking too early about the writing sequence interferes with students' thinking about their own prior knowledge and the information in the texts. Now that students have thought through and organized this foundational thinking, they are ready to lay out the sequence for the essay (2002, 151-152).

Writing instruction within the social studies discipline should not focus exclusively on developing students' ability to write persuasive or argumentative essays. By its nature, social studies content often lends itself to discussions concerning point of view, role playing, civics, equality, and law.

Ventre (1979) provides the following example of a social studies lesson that emphasizes writing and strives to improve students' use of voice and awareness of audience. The assignment was created for an American history class, but can be adapted for any grade level and topic of study without changing the emphasis on voice and audience. The lesson includes the following steps:

1) Students read items by and about John Brown, an important figure in the time just before the outbreak of the Civil War.

2) Together, the class develops a list of information and observations on the chalkboard under two headings: *John Brown—Hero/John Brown—Villain*

3) Each student writes a letter about John Brown using the following method:

   • Each student chooses a character from a list of paired opposites. For example, Rhett, a Southern newspaper reporter supporting African colonization, and Hans, a Northern editor who came to America seeking political refuge.

   • Each student then writes a three-paragraph letter from that character to the other character of the pair. The letter should defend the appropriate point of view of that character toward John Brown—as either hero or villain.

4) During the next class, students exchange and discuss their letters with a student who has written from the perspective of the opposite member of the pair.

Social studies should not be about simply memorizing dates and names. By assuming the viewpoint of a character who lived during the time period under study, it is possible for students to gain a better understanding of the atmosphere, tensions, and issues of the time. Students will find the subject matter more interesting when they are able to understand how people like themselves lived, felt, and reacted to certain situations. This viewpoint is critical to understanding history, and writing provides a good vehicle for obtaining and expressing this viewpoint.

Recognizing cause-and-effect relationships and distinguishing fact from opinion are two other skills often taught in social studies classes that lend themselves to writing assignments. Teachers can help students recognize cause-and-effect relationships by calling attention to signal words in expository writing, such as "because," "therefore," "so," and "in order to" (Hickey 1990). After a class discussion of this concept, students can be asked to read about an event and to describe the cause-and-effect relationship in their own words. This exercise will encourage students to think critically about what they have read, as well as promote their understanding of cause-and-effect relationships.

In order to help students distinguish fact from opinion, teachers could ask students to analyze newspaper articles, examine the statements presented in them, and determine which ones are verifiable facts. Students can then be asked to restate factual information as opinion, and opinion as fact (Hickey 1990). A writing exercise might involve students role-playing the part of a reporter who has witnessed an event, and then writing two articles on what he/she has seen—one which is fact and one which is opinion.

Social studies is not just about studying history—it is also an opportunity to learn about civics. Stotsky (1994) describes the many ways in which students can use their reading and writing abilities to promote civic responsibility. She writes, "Civic writing ranges from petitions and letters of opinion to editors and legislators, to the many kinds of writing, such as agendas and minutes of meetings, needed for organizing and maintaining democratically run citizen boards and other civic or political organizations" (172).

Peggy Carwin, a seventh-grade teacher, had her students send letters to a local nursing home offering their services to patients. She also asked them to write thank-you letters to officials at local newspapers and companies that helped provide for the distribution of newspapers to their school for National Literacy Day, as well as letters to their local congressman requesting new American flags for their school (Stotsky 1994).

How Can Writing Be Included Effectively in the Social Studies Curriculum?

The most effective method of using writing to both enhance learning and encourage creative and critical thinking appears to be the development and use of writing assignments that stimulate and challenge students. Four categories of assignments can be identified:

1. *Reporting*. Students are directed to compile information with a minimum of critical or original thinking. Example: Write a report on the outbreak and major events of the Spanish-American War.

2. *Exposition*. Students are asked to explain an idea, conduct a critical investigation, synthesize issues, or bring a fresh point of view to a problem. Example: Write an essay to compare and contrast the views of U.S. citizens who wanted to annex the Philippines in 1898 and those who opposed the annexation.

3. *Narration*. Students are asked to tell a story, an anecdote, tall tale, legend, short story, drama, or vignette. Example: Pretend you are a soldier with Teddy Roosevelt's Rough Riders. Write an article for your hometown newspaper about the charge up San Juan Hill that combines some fiction with actual facts about the battle.

4. *Argumentation*. Students are asked to evaluate, defend, or attack an idea or belief. Example: After reading the speech by Senator Beveridge of Indiana supporting the annexation of the Philippines, write a speech supporting or attacking his position. Support your arguments (Risinger 1987, online).

Chapter Six

Assessment of Student Writing: Purposes, Approaches, and Tools

Assessment is a vital tool in any effective instructional program. Good assessments provide data to help teachers determine the current knowledge and skills that individual students possess, while also helping students self-assess their own skills. Strickland et al. (2002) talk about this: "Assessment should acknowledge what . . . [students] are doing well, while helping them make informed decisions about what they need to work on" (197). When analyzed and interpreted, the information generated by assessments can be used as the basis for crucial instructional decisions about pacing, remediation, and the introduction of new information, as well as staff development and program design.

Because assessment of student progress is key to ensuring that instruction is both on-target and effective, school and classroom assessment activities should be a carefully planned component of the instructional framework. For teachers in content-area classes who are providing students with opportunities to write, the task becomes more complex since the assessments used address both content-area and writing competencies.

Why Assess Student Writing?

Assessment of student writing can serve many purposes, and an understanding of these purposes can help teachers choose an appropriate assessment approach. For example, when evaluation includes the assignment of grades, teachers have a convenient vehicle for reporting student performance and progress to students, parents, and others. When a teacher provides comments and corrections, students receive valuable feedback that can improve future efforts. Additional purposes for writing assessment include:

- *Highlighting assessment as a meaning-making process.* Approaches that serve this purpose put a premium on engaging students in writing and encourage creativity, personal response, and interpretation. They have potential to promote better learning and a more in-depth understanding of subject matter.

- *Providing teachers with diagnostic information about a student's writing ability.* Approaches that serve this purpose might be used to inform the instruction of students who have particular writing weaknesses. Once a student's strengths and weaknesses have been identified, the instructor can determine which strategies might address the weaknesses.

Managing Assessment of Student Writing

There are a number of ways to order and manage the volume of paperwork created by writing activities. Pugalee et al. offer the following suggestions:

- Pre-assign students to pairs or heterogeneous groups of four or five and allow them to "put their heads together" in the composition of a single written product, called "communal writing."

- Have several students volunteer to read their work aloud in class to promote class discussion or obtain teacher feedback.

- Develop a system of reading student writing so that over a two-week period each student receives extensive feedback about selected pieces of writing.

- Select random pieces of writing and provide a summary of strengths and weaknesses as part of the next class (or skim all work to generate a summary).

- Engage the students in peer editing, where students assume various roles such as editor, proofreader, recorder, or reader.

- Read responses and write one brief comment for each student.

- Develop scoring rubrics for peer, teacher, or self-assessment (1999, 51).

Assessment as a Meaning-Making Process

As reading and writing have come to be viewed as interactive processes involving a transaction between the reader/writer and the text, parallel evaluation methods have been developed. One example is portfolio assessment, in which students create portfolios of written work that include items such as their personal responses to reading assignments. The rationale behind these new types of assessment is that because reading and writing are dynamic processes, they require a dynamic form of assessment.

This is not to say, however, that quizzes and standardized tests are without value. There are instances when a quiz can be useful, such as when a teacher needs a quick method of determining how much students have understood from the text. The new emphasis on assessment as a meaning-making process, however, stands in sharp contrast to the traditional definition of assessment as something produced after the learning has occurred, in order to measure what has been learned. This new perspective stresses that assessment should be part of the learning process, not separate from it. Learning can occur while students are creating something that will be assessed, as well as once they receive teacher feedback on the product they have created.

Although assessment methods that emphasize meaning-making—such as essay writing, portfolios, and personal anthologies—may seem more relevant for English classes than for content-area classes, most can be easily adapted for content-area assignments. For example, portfolios are now being used more and more in math classes; these portfolios might include student-formulated problems or samples of journal writing related to mathematical concepts being studied (Crowley 1993).

A few ideas for assessing student learning through writing activities are described below. Note that each involves writing and can be used to evaluate students' subject matter knowledge as well as their writing ability. Each method is appropriate for language arts assessment and also can be applied in the content areas.

- *Continuation of a story*. Have students continue the plot after the end of the story, by describing what happens to the main character.

- *Point of view*. Have students rewrite the material from the point of view of another character who was not a narrator. In mathematics class, this could involve describing an alternate solution to a problem.

- *Rewrite the ending*. Students often have their own ideas about how a story, either fiction or nonfiction, should have ended. Rewriting can be done individually or by groups creating scripts; the scripts can then be acted out for the rest of the class.

- *Newspapers*. Students can write newspaper articles about an event or several events in the text or historical occurrence. These can be interviews, feature articles, or photo essays. The articles might have to do with the discovery of a new chemical, conducting a population census, tallying votes during an election, or finding a new vaccine.

- *Relating material to themselves*. For example, if students in a science class were reading about efforts to develop a polio vaccine, they might compare this to how they feel about efforts to find a cure for a modern-day illness.

- *Scripting a meeting of characters*. Students can be asked to imagine that four individuals from the historical time period under study have gathered in one place. Working in small groups, they imagine what would happen and create a script. They perform the script in front of classmates, and then write reflective essays on their experience working on this project (Tuley 1994).

Student projects should be evaluated on the basis of how consistent they are with the material presented and on whether students have considered relevant concepts, issues, and events. Naturally, some forms of evaluation will work better with some material than others. For example, a story or historical event with a controversial ending would be particularly appropriate for an assignment to rewrite the ending.

Using Rubrics to Assess Student Writing

In addition to providing information about student mastery of content-area material, many samples of student writing simultaneously provide a means of assessing student competencies related to writing. Strickland and Morrow write that the goal of assessing students' writing is "to uncover the child's knowledge about written language, which will guide the teacher in planning instruction for the child" (2000, 164).

While teachers may understand the importance of evaluating student writing, many are unsure about what to look for as they read student essays. They may wonder whether to focus on content, voice, structure, or grammatical correctness. To complicate matters, grading of written work often varies from teacher to teacher, making it difficult for students to focus on and practice critical elements. A key to effective writing instruction can be rubrics, which are embedded in both instruction and assessment.

Rubrics serve as an effective way to communicate expectations and also can be used to assist teachers in evaluating student writing samples (Walley and Kommer 2000). In addition to ensuring that teachers apply assessment criteria consistently across students, rubrics allow students to see the criteria on which they will be graded. Teachers, when assigning a writing task that will be evaluated with a rubric, should share the rubric with their students and explain to them how the task will be evaluated and the specific proficiencies they will be expected to demonstrate. Rubrics often vary in design, but all include the criteria of the assignment, the indicators describing how the criteria will be met, and a rating scale.

6+1 Traits of Student Writing

The Northwest Regional Educational Laboratory has developed a framework known as 6+1 Trait Writing, which is designed to create a common vision of what "good writing" looks like and to pinpoint students' strengths and weaknesses in writing (2001, online). Detailed information on this rubric-based approach can be downloaded from www.nwrel.org/assessment/pdfRubrics/6plus1traits.

Listed below are the major categories in the 6+1 approach, accompanied by a description of what a well-developed piece of writing would look like from each perspective.

Ideas/Content: The ideas are the heart of the message, the content of the piece, the main theme, together with the details that enrich and develop that theme.

- The topic is narrow and manageable.

- Relevant, telling, quality details give the reader important information that goes beyond the obvious or predictable.

- The reader's questions are anticipated and answered.

Organization: Organization is the internal structure of a piece of writing, the thread of central meaning, the logical and sometimes intriguing pattern of the ideas.

- An inviting introduction draws the reader in; a satisfying conclusion leaves the reader with a sense of closure and resolution.

- Thoughtful transitions clearly show how ideas connect.

- Details seem to fit where they're placed; sequencing is logical and effective.

- Pacing is well-controlled; the writer knows when to slow down and elaborate, and when to pick up the pace and move on.

Voice: The voice is the heart and soul, the magic, the wit, along with the feeling and conviction of the individual writer coming out through the words.

- The tone of the writing adds interest to the message and is appropriate for the purpose and audience.

- Expository or persuasive writing reflects a strong commitment to the topic by showing why the reader needs to know this and why he or she should care.

- Narrative writing is honest, personal, and engaging and makes the reader think about, and react to, the author's ideas and point of view.

Word Choice: Word choice is the use of rich, colorful, precise language that moves and enlightens the reader.

- Words are specific and accurate. It is easy to understand just what the writer means.

- Language and phrasing is natural, effective, and appropriate for the audience.

- Choices in language enhance the meaning and clarify understanding.

Sentence Fluency: Sentence fluency is the rhythm and flow of the language, the sound of word patterns, the way in which the writing plays to the ear— not just to the eye.

- Sentences are constructed in a way that underscores and enhances the meaning.

- Sentences vary in length as well as structure. Fragments, if used, add style. Dialogue, if present, sounds natural.

- The writing has cadence; the writer has thought about the sounds of words as well as the meaning.

Conventions/Mechanics: Conventions are the mechanical correctness of the piece—the spelling, grammar and usage, paragraphing, use of capitals, and punctuation.

- Spelling is generally correct, even on more difficult words.

- The punctuation is accurate, even creative, and guides the reader through the text.

- Grammar and usage are correct and contribute to clarity and style.

- Paragraphing tends to be sound and reinforces the organizational structure.

+1 Presentation: Presentation zeros in on the form and layout of the text and its readability; the piece should be pleasing to the eye.

- If handwritten (rather than cursive or printed), the slant is consistent, letters are clearly formed, spacing is uniform between words, and the text is easy to read.

- If word-processed, there is appropriate use of fonts and font sizes which invites the reader into the text.

- The use of white space on the page (spacing, margins, etc.) allows the intended audience to easily focus on the text and message without distractions. There is just the right amount of balance of white space and text on the page. The formatting suits the purpose for writing (Northwest Regional Educational Laboratory n.d., online).

Other Rubrics for Writing

The key to effective use of rubrics is not simply their content. Instead, it is important that rubrics be well-aligned with the task, have meaning for students, and can be applied consistently. Included on the next two pages are two additional rubric-based approaches that teachers can use to develop their own approaches to evaluating student writing.

Involving Students in Developing Criteria Charts

To assist students in evaluating their own writing and identifying their strengths and weaknesses, involve them in developing criteria for self-assessment. Some of these criteria are based on rubrics of what good writing looks like; others focus on the process of good writing.

Criteria for Evaluating Student Writing

	4	3	2	1
Development of topic	Original, interesting development of topic	Acceptable development of topic	Attempts to develop topic but shows weaknesses	Lacks plan to develop topic
Organization and Use of Support Material	Full development of ideas through excellent use of support material	Adequate use of support material to develop ideas	Little use of support material to develop ideas	Does not use support material to develop ideas
Sentence Variety	Skillful use of sentence variety	Some sentence variety	Little sentence variety	Lack of sentence variety
Language	Uses rich vocabulary and images	Uses general language	Uses incorrect language	Frequently uses incorrect language
Conventions	Few or no errors	Errors do not interfere with meaning	Errors interfere with meaning	Errors seriously interfere with meaning

Source: Scala 2001, 36.

Rubric for Evaluating Student Writing

Score of 6

A paper in this category demonstrates clear and consistent competence, though it may have occasional errors. Such a paper:

· effectively and insightfully addresses the writing task;
· is well organized and fully developed, using clearly appropriate examples to support ideas; and
· displays consistent facility in the use of language, demonstrating variety in sentence structure and range of vocabulary.

Score of 5

A paper in this category demonstrates reasonably consistent competence, though it will have occasional errors or lapses in quality. Such a paper:

· effectively addresses the writing task;
· is generally well organized and well developed, using appropriate examples to support ideas; and
· displays facility in the use of language, demonstrating some syntactic variety and range of vocabulary.

Score of 4

A paper in this category demonstrates adequate competence with occasional errors and lapses in quality. Such a paper:

· addresses the writing task;
· is organized and adequately developed, using examples to support ideas;
· displays adequate but inconsistent facility in the use of language, presenting some errors in grammar or diction; and
· presents minimal sentence variety.

Score of 3

A paper in this category demonstrates developing competence. Such a paper may contain one or more of the following weaknesses:

· inadequate organization or development;
· inappropriate or insufficient details to support ideas; and
· an accumulation of errors in grammar, diction, or sentence structure.

Score of 2

A paper in this category demonstrates some competence. Such a paper is flawed by one or more of the following weaknesses:

· poor organization;
· poor development;
· little or inappropriate detail to support ideas; and
· frequent errors in grammar, diction, and sentence structure.

Score of 1

A paper in this category demonstrates incompetence. Such a paper is seriously flawed by one or more of the following weaknesses:

· very poor organization;
· very thin development; and
· usage and syntactical errors so severe that meaning is somewhat obscured (The College Board n.d., online).

In order to help her students look at writing from both these perspectives, a teacher asked her students two questions: "What do good writers do?" and "What makes writing good?" As students voiced their suggestions, the teacher wrote their ideas on chart paper. She demonstrated to her students that their answers fell into three categories—writing process; qualities of good writing; and grammar, spelling, and mechanics—and helped her students sort their responses into these categories. After this session, the teacher copied the chart onto poster board and displayed it in the classroom for students to use as a reference. (See the Classroom Writing Criteria Chart below.)

Classroom Writing Criteria Chart:
What Do Good Writers Do?

Writing Process	Qualities of Good Writing	Grammar, Spelling, and Mechanics
• Choose a good topic • Keep a journal • Confer with the teacher • Confer with other students • Use revision strategies • Make several drafts • Share what they write	• Include beginning, middle, and end • Start sentences in different ways • Use powerful verbs • Use lots of details • Make sure it makes sense	• Check spelling • Check for capitals at beginning of sentences • Write neatly (Strickland et al. 2002, 198).

To assess their writing, students were given a T-chart (see the next page) on which they recorded at least one thing from each of the three categories of process, content, and mechanics that they were doing well and one thing from each category that they needed to work on. Students kept their T-charts in their writing folders and referred to them over several weeks as the teacher helped each of them focus on areas identified as needing more work (Strickland, Ganske, and Monroe 2002).

Student Self-Evaluation T-Chart

Things I am doing well in writing	One thing I need to work on

Source: Strickland, Ganske, and Monroe 2002, 199.

Chapter Seven

Helping Struggling Writers

Literacy levels vary greatly at the middle and high school levels, especially when it comes to students' writing ability. It is not uncommon for some students in a classroom to be writing lengthy, well-developed essays, while others struggle to develop a coherent paragraph. Teachers must address this range of ability levels in their instruction, and support students at the "struggling" end of the continuum as they strive to improve their writing—while at the same time focusing on content-area instruction.

Stein, Dixon, and Barnard use the term *struggling* or *reluctant* writers to refer to "those students who lack important knowledge and skills necessary for effective written communication, those students who frequently experience failure when required to express themselves in writing" (2001, 107-8). They note there are many reasons why students may experience difficulty performing writing tasks: they may have been taught using less effective curricula; they may have lacked opportunities for practice; or they may have learning problems that inhibit their learning to write well (2001).

In addition, Isaacson notes struggling writers "may have difficulty with memory problems, poor selective attention, lack of mechanical skills, insufficient procedural strategies, and poor metacognitive skills as well as the inability to assume another's perspective" (in Stein, Dixon, and Barnard 2001, 108). Raphael and Englert add that struggling writers also may exhibit these characteristics:

- an inability to sustain their thinking about topics;

- poor organizational skills;

- insensitivity to audience needs (e.g., not setting contexts, no use of text signals);

- failure to provide a purpose;

- inability to perceive themselves as informants with information to share; and

- poor use of conventions of print (1990, 389).

For other students, perfectionism may be a stumbling block. As Roush writes, some students "want to write as well as the authors they most admire, but they despair of attaining the high standards they set for themselves. Sometimes low self-esteem is the problem. They find it almost impossible to believe that anyone else would value their stories" (1992, 29).

The Texas Center for Reading and Language Arts presents characteristics of effective and struggling writers (see these on the following page) and suggests teachers consider where individual students lie along a continuum of these characteristics. In the view of the Center, a goal for teachers should be moving students in the direction of effective practices.

Given the wide range of factors that may contribute to students' writing difficulties and the range of student abilities within a classroom, what can teachers do to help students who struggle with writing?

Research points to the positive impact of engaging all students—regardless of writing ability—in writing activities every day (Wood and Shea-Bischoff 1997; Rhodes and Dudley-Marling 1996; Routmann 1996). These writing experiences do not need to be long or formal, but they must be meaningful. Wood and Shea-Bischoff assert that "the only way students will improve their writing skill is to practice writing as much as possible" (1997, 50). They stress that these experiences do not need to be graded or "edited to perfection"— rather, they should be viewed as "practice writing sessions" that can be integrated into all areas of the curriculum (50). Many of the writing activities described in Chapter 4 meet this criterion and can be used for this purpose. In addition, "informal" techniques also should be used to encourage students to write for any purpose, whether to make a list, jot down notes, write a letter to a pen pal, or brainstorm thoughts.

Even with daily opportunities to write and high-quality instruction, however, some students may need additional assistance to become proficient writers. This assistance will have a greater impact if it is provided across content areas instead of being limited to time in language arts classes. The remainder of this chapter presents some practical and specific strategies for helping students with writing difficulties.

	Effective Writers	**Struggling Writers**
Motivational characteristics	• Willing to take risks • Value writing for communication and enjoyment • Have experienced some prior success • Confident that they have something worthwhile to say	• Lack confidence and avoid risks • Have little intrinsic motivation for writing • Fail to understand or appreciate writing's purpose in their lives
Knowledge and skills	• Understand and apply fundamental rules of grammar, syntax, punctuation, and spelling • Have a well-developed vocabulary • Have knowledge of sentence and text structure	• Do not know the characteristics of good writing • Have little knowledge of text structure • Lack lower- and higher-order writing skills • Have a limited vocabulary • Have difficulty with the rules of grammar, syntax, punctuation, and spelling
Processes	• Use a recursive writing process, moving freely among planning, drafting, and revising • Engage in knowledge transformation to ideas, concepts • Self-monitor and reflect upon product and processes • Possess a repertoire of writing strategies	• Write in linear fashion, fail to rethink initial decisions and attempts • Engage in "knowledge telling," stating facts • Fail to monitor effectiveness of product or processes • Lack strategies for improving their writing
Written products	• Show a clear sense of audience and purpose • Are well organized and coherent • Use appropriate grammar, syntax, punctuation, spelling, and word choice • Convey clear expression of ideas • Use well-developed, appropriate elaboration	• Are shorter in length • Lack coherence • Have missing critical parts • Are riddled with mechanical and grammatical errors (Texas Center for Reading and Language Arts 2000, 4-6).

Making the Writing Experience Less Threatening

While some students—especially those who are already effective writers—have no difficulty in deciding what to write, this first step may be a major stumbling block to other students. Given this, teachers should help students learn how to independently choose topics.

Marchisan and Alber (2001) suggest one way to help students begin to feel more comfortable with this task is to provide opportunities for them to talk about their favorite activities and then pick one aspect to describe in a paragraph. The focus in the exercise should not be limited to the content of student writing but on the process of how they moved from conversation to the written word. They also suggest students be taught to routinely ask themselves questions such as:

1) Why am I writing (purpose)?

2) What will I write about (subject)?

3) What will I say (content)?

4) How will I say it (voice)?

5) For whom am I writing (audience)? (Marchisan and Alber 2001).

The following strategies may be useful in assisting students during the prewriting stage of the writing process—and in helping them understand how to address this task independently:

Wordless Picture Books. Although most commonly used at the elementary level, wordless picture books also have their place in the middle and high school classroom. Wordless picture books can serve as a great stimulus for writing, as students can "read" the pictures and develop text that reflects what the picture represents. Wordless picture books also can be used to help students choose writing topics and to teach them to "think like an author." Content-area teachers can develop short wordless picture books by copying illustrations from the text or related instructional materials—or by downloading pictures from the Web. These need not be limited to "stories," but can also be used, for example, to graphically illustrate a scientific process.

Wood and Shea-Bischoff recommend the following sequence of steps when introducing wordless picture books in an upper grades classroom:

1) Introduce students to the world of wordless picture books by showing the work of various authors. Tell them that the reason these books do not have words is to enable the "readers" to invent their own story lines.

2) Walk them through a book and ask them to orally tell what they think is going on in the pictures. You may need to "think aloud" your own version of the first few pages to model this new experience for them. For this modeling portion, it may be helpful to put the book on over-head transparencies if it is being used with a large group of students.

3) Then, beginning with the first page, ask students to tell you in sentence form what they think should be written on that page. Write their sentences underneath the picture on the transparency. Encourage the use of dialogue when appropriate and tell the students "to think like an author" since they are, in essence, writing their own book.

4) After completing the last page, return to the beginning and ask the students to read the book in its completed form. This may be done chorally, in pairs, or individually depending upon the needs of the students.

5) This book can be duplicated for each group member and used repeatedly to foster fluency (smoothness of reading) and to provide additional practice with high frequency words (words that appear every third or fourth word in our language) (1997, 51).

Playful Writing. Weber (2000) suggests that adding "playfulness" to a writing assignment motivates students while also stretching their thinking beyond normal expectations and encouraging them to combine ideas that are typically not associated with one another. Suggestions for playful writing topics include: "describing pet peeves, inventing phobias for common experiences (like sistaphobia—fear of sisters), retelling embarrassing situations with family members or friends, and writing a futuristic obituary" (Weber 2000, 564). In addition, playful writing might include the use of repetition, exaggeration, and unexpected association (Weber 2000).

Some Common Problems

Strong et al. describe some common problems associated with student writing, along with suggestions for addressing them. For example, if the writing product:

- is minimal in terms of content, the student may need help with the "how-to's" of collecting information. Strategies to help a student develop related skills include:

    - *Generating questions*. Student generates a list of questions that will help the reader understand the topic, then reads and takes notes on which questions were answered and which still need answering.

    - *Visualizing*. Student visualizes, then draws ideas related to task and topic. Drawing becomes the basis for brainstorming.

    - *Peer collection*. Student talks to a peer on what she knows/ thinks she knows/needs to know. Peer takes notes that guide students through reading. Students re-pair to discuss what the writing will be like.

- often wanders off on tangents, the student may need help with organizing information. Strategies to help a student develop related skills include:

    - *Fat Ts*. Student draws several "Fat Ts." In the top of the T she writes a main idea she wants to communicate. In the base, she lists supporting details. Student numbers Ts in order for writing.

    - *Grouping*. Student brainstorms all she might include in her writing, then places items that go together into groups. Student labels each group and decides on its order.

    - *Peer organization*. Student organizes notes into a beginning, middle, and end. She tells a friend about her piece and asks the friend to take notes and to help find out which parts were hard to understand.

- spends too much time on obvious or unnecessary information or assumes background information not commonly known, the student may need help with evaluating his/her own work. Strategies to help a student develop related skills include:

    - *Clarifying purpose*. Without looking at her piece, the student writes notes on what she meant to say in the beginning, middle, and end. Then she reads the piece, looking for places where she did not communicate what she meant to say and revising accordingly.

- *Imagining a reader*. Student imagines what she wants her reader to feel or think about each section of her piece and makes notes on it. Then, she reads her piece to a friend, asks what the friend thinks and feels about each section, and makes notes. She uses her notes to develop a revision plan.

- *Reading aloud*. Student has a partner read her own piece to her and makes notes on words, phrases, or sentences that sound clumsy. These notes become the basis for revision (excerpted from Strong et al. 2002, 153-54.)

Addressing the Mechanics of Writing

During the writing stage, students put their thoughts on paper in the form of sentences and paragraphs. Their work at this stage should expand upon their prewriting plan notes. While preparing their first draft, students should not be concerned with grammar or spelling—the goal is simply for them to record their ideas. Teachers can help by providing support that helps struggling writers focus on the task—for example, by providing wordbanks of words relevant to the topic, by having students write with partners, or by encouraging students to develop notes and a first draft using a word processing program.

Using Technology to Support Students

Technology provides another tool that can be especially useful for students struggling with writing, especially if students are taught to use technology to allow them to focus on the content—rather than the mechanics—of writing. For example, the Texas Center for Reading and Language Arts suggests students should be taught to use word processing programs to:

- organize and reorganize their written thoughts during the planning stage;

- develop outlines using the conventional form or a software organizational tool; and

- make changes to their text as they generate new ideas (2000, 30).

Some students who struggle with writing experience difficulties that go beyond the logical expression of ideas, choosing a topic, or writing for an audience. Some students may have trouble with hand-eye coordination or have trouble physically holding and writing with a pencil, while others may be very slow at putting their thoughts down on paper. For these students, the computer substantially reduces the frustration of making revisions and recopying. Research suggests that the key to fluent writing is to write as much as possible—the computer makes it easier for students to do this (Simic 1994). Simic provides specific details on the benefits of student use of computers while writing:

> Word processing allows rapid alteration and manipulation of the text, helping writers sustain the mental images they are trying to capture while experimenting with language. The search/replace capability encourages synonym substitution, and the immediate access to a clean copy stimulates further language play (1994, online).

Technology can help students learn to become better writers in another way—through the easy availability of Web-based resources on writing. For example, dozens of links to resources suitable for middle and high school students on the writing process can be found at www.angelfire.com/wi/writingprocess/secwplinks.html.

Helping Students Learn How to Evaluate Their Own Work

Marchisan and Alber describe the editing and revision stage of the writing process as the time when "students evaluate the strengths and weaknesses of the form and content of their writing piece and make changes based on these judgements" (2001, 158). Strategies used while students edit and revise their own work should assist them in viewing the drafts as the intended audience might, even if the product is intended to be more informal. The following strategies can be especially useful with students who need extra support:

- *Provide a self-evaluation checklist.* To guide students through the editing and revision process, provide them with a list of questions to answer as they read through their first draft. (Sample checklists for revising fiction and nonfiction are provided on page 88.) Marchisan and Alber (2001) suggest the checklists should include questions related to content, organization, and style. In order to get the most out of the exercise, they also suggest students should be taught to

Merritt provides some writing instruction-related suggestions for teachers who are working with ESL students:

> In terms of language conventions, it is helpful for teachers to avoid correcting every single error and instead focus energy on errors that are most likely to cloud meaning. Also, rather than engaging students in "skill and drill" with decontextualized exercises, teachers can help students look at the errors in their writing in terms of patterns which can be learned and applied. ESL students will eventually self-correct if the teacher models appropriate vocabulary and grammar.
>
> When teaching writing to ESL students, however, teachers need to go beyond just language conventions and help writers build confidence. One way to help them build confidence is to make them familiar with the conventions of the kinds of writing they will be doing in the class....
>
> Teachers can help ESL students understand conventions of English not only by pointing them out and modeling them but by engaging students in discussion about writing in their native language. Likewise, ESL students benefit from many opportunities to use English through speaking and writing in a literacy rich environment.
>
> The most valuable things that teachers can do to help their ESL students' writing are engage them in writing-to-learn activities, help them find patterns in their errors to help them feel that they can learn language conventions, include illustrations/graphics for novice ESL students, and give them opportunities to talk about their writing and course content (2003, 26).

write notes on their drafts as they evaluate and to go back to these notes as they revise.

- *Peer response*. This strategy for revision pairs students together to read and comment on one another's written work. Graham and Harris write, "With peer reponse children provide suggestions to each

Revision Checklists

Revising Fiction

Title _____

Author _____

Date _____

Peer Editor _____

- Is the beginning interesting?
- Does the story make sense?
- Are the characters believable? Do they act like real people?
- Do the characters use conversation?
- Are the character's personalities developed?
- Does the story have a problem that needs to be solved?
- Are the descriptions of the scenes clear?
- Does each scene build toward the high point (climax) of the story?
- Is there an exciting or high point of the story?
- Is the conclusion logical? Does it wrap up all the loose ends?
- Was the conflict or problem resolved?
- Was there a moral or theme?

Revising Nonfiction

Title _____

Author _____

Date _____

Peer Editor _____

- Has the author written for a particular audience?
- Has the author written for a specific purpose?
- Does the introduction to the piece get the reader involved right away?
- Are the ideas developed in a logical sequence?
- Does the author stay on topic?
- Are the ideas clear?
- Are there details to support the main ideas?
- Is correct grammar used?
- Are words spelled correctly?
- Is there a surprise ending or strong conclusion? (Marchisan and Alber 2001, 158).

other on how to improve their first drafts using a structured format" (1999, 262). After students have completed an initial draft, they read their work to a writing partner who listens and reads along. Once the paper has been read, the partner summarizes what the story or writing is about and indicates the two or three things he/she liked best about the paper. The partner then rereads the paper or story, asking him/herself these questions: "Is there any place that isn't clear?" and "Is there any place that more detail could be added?" (Graham and Harris 1999, 262). After this is completed, the paper is returned to the author, and the students discuss any necessary revisions. Then, the author revises his/her paper using the partner's comments as a guide. When the other student has prepared an initial draft, the two students will meet together again to share in the revision process.

Depending on specific student needs, any combination of the strategies illustrated throughout this text can help improve student-writing abilities. Further, these techniques can be altered to fit most any range of student literacy levels—struggling and proficient writers alike.

Chapter Eight

Taking a Schoolwide Approach

Stephens and Brown suggest that integrating writing instruction in the content areas should be considerd "neither an add-on to the curriculum, nor is it a substitute for content. It provides teachers and students alike with effective tools for learning the content of any subject" (2000, 9). Through their support for the development of student writing skills in all classes, school leaders demonstrate their understanding that writing instruction in the content areas is neither an add-on nor a substitute—but simply good teaching.

By helping students to become effective readers and writers, teachers are actually helping their students master content-area material, as proficiency in reading and writing skills is necessary for content-area learning. But teachers should also realize that, even at the middle and high school levels, some students will need additional instruction designed to strengthen and improve their writing. Stephens and Brown point to this: "A dramatic shift occurs for many students, however, when they enter middle school or high school. Frequently, it is assumed that students can write analytical responses to reading informational texts. The differences between writing stories and using expository modes to inform, describe, persuade, explain, or critique too often remain untaught" (2000, 5). This is often referred to as "writing to learn" and exemplifies the difference between "writing to learn" and "learning to write."

Thus, teachers' responses to the question "Why should I provide opportunities for students to write?" should address the need to help students "write to learn"—to help them use writing as a tool for learning subject matter. Teachers who make writing to learn a priority and incorporate the teaching of reading and writing strategies into their content-area instruction understand how students learn.

Principals and assistant principals have roles to play in helping students develop as effective writers. Obviously, an important consideration for school leaders as well as teachers is student performance on state-required

The goal of instruction should be "to help students learn content while developing the literacy and thinking skills necessary to become independent, lifelong learners" (Stephens and Brown 2000, 2).

assessments. Providing effective writing-related instruction and opportunities for students to write across the curriculum can enhance the possibility that typically low-achieving students reach standards on this often-difficult portion of the assessment.

While each state has slightly different expectations for its students in regard to writing competency, the description of NAEP Basic, Proficient, and Advanced levels for eighth and 12th grades (see pages 93 and 94) provides a reminder of the challenge of helping all students develop as writers. Although fourth-and eighth-graders demonstrated slight improvements on the 2002 assessment as compared to 1998, twelfth-graders' achievement remained stagnant. In addition, there are too many students performing at the Below Basic and Basic Levels (see table below), with too few at the Proficient or Advanced levels. Both the descriptions of the competencies needed for the more advanced levels and the current levels of performance demonstrate the challenges ahead for many schools.

Percentage of Students, by NAEP 2002 Writing Achievement Level, Grades 4, 8, and 12

	Below Basic	At Basic	At Proficient	At Advanced
Grade 4	14%	58%	26%	2%
Grade 8	15	54	29	2
Grade 12	26	51	22	2

(Persky, Daane, and Jin 2003, 21)

Principals can help by enlisting all teachers in the effort to help students learn more effective writing skills—and by providing the support teachers need to do this. For example, a schoolwide emphasis on student writing can be supported by:

Descriptions of NAEP Writing Achievement Levels, Grade 8

Student performances reported with respect to these descriptions are in response to two age-appropriate writing tasks completed within 25 minutes each. Students are not advised of the writing tasks in advance nor engaged in pre-writing instruction and preparation; however, they are given a set of "ideas for planning and reviewing" their writing for the assessment. Although the Writing NAEP cannot fully assess students' abilities to produce a polished piece of writing, the results do provide valuable information about students' abilities to generate writing in response to a variety of purposes, tasks, and audiences within a rather limited period of time.

Eighth-grade students performing at the Basic level should be able to produce an effective response within the time allowed that shows a general understanding of the writing task they have been assigned. Their writing should show that these students are aware of the audience they are expected to address, and it should include supporting details in an organized way. The grammar, spelling, punctuation, and capitalization in the work should be accurate enough to communicate to a reader, although there may be mistakes that get in the way of meaning.

Eighth-grade students performing at the Proficient level should be able to produce an effective response within the time allowed that shows an understanding of both the writing task they have been assigned and the audience they are expected to address. Their writing should be organized, making use of techniques such as sequencing or a clearly marked beginning and ending, and it should make use of details and some elaboration to support and develop the main idea of the piece. Their writing should include precise language and some variety in sentence structure, and it may show analytical, evaluative, or creative thinking. The grammar, spelling, punctuation, and capitalization in the work should be accurate enough to communicate to a reader; there may be some errors, but these should not get in the way of meaning.

Eighth-grade students performing at the Advanced level should be able to produce an effective and fully developed response within the time allowed that shows a clear understanding of both the writing task they have been assigned and the audience they are expected to address. Their writing should show some analytical, evaluative, or creative thinking, and should demonstrate precise word choice and varied sentence structure. Their work should include details and elaboration that support and develop the main idea of the piece, and it may make use of strategies such as analogies, illustrations, examples, anecdotes, or figurative language to clarify a point. At the same time, the writing should show that these students can keep their work clearly and consistently organized. Writing by eighth-grade students performing at the Advanced level should contain few errors in grammar, spelling, punctuation, capitalization, and sentence structure. These writers should demonstrate good control of these elements and may use them for stylistic effect in their work (Excerpted from Persky, Daane, and Jin 2003, 11).

Descriptions of NAEP Writing
Achievement Levels, Grade 12

Student performances reported with respect to these descriptions are in response to two age-appropriate writing tasks completed within 25 minutes each. Students are not advised of the writing tasks in advance nor engaged in pre-writing instruction and preparation; however, they are given a set of "ideas for planning and reviewing" their writing for the assessment.

Twelfth-grade students performing at the Basic level should be able to produce an effective response . . . that shows an understanding of both the writing task they have been assigned and the audience they are expected to address. Their writing should show some analytical, evaluative, or creative thinking. It should include details that support and develop the central idea of the piece, and it should be clearly organized . . . grammar, spelling, punctuation, and capitalization in these students' work should be accurate enough to communicate to a reader; there may be some errors, but these should not get in the way of meaning.

Twelfth-grade students performing at the Proficient level should be able to produce an effective and fully developed response . . . that uses analytical, evaluative, or creative thinking. Their writing should be organized effectively, and it should show that these students have a clear understanding of the writing task they have been assigned. It should be coherent, making use of techniques such as a consistent theme, sequencing, and a clear introduction and conclusion, and it should include details and elaboration that support and develop the main idea of the piece . . .writing by twelfth-grade students performing at the Proficient level should contain few errors in grammar, spelling, punctuation, capitalization, and sentence structure. These writers should demonstrate a command of these elements and may use them for stylistic effect in their work.

Twelfth-grade students performing at the Advanced level should be able to produce a mature and sophisticated response . . .that uses analytical, evaluative, or creative thinking. Their writing should be fully developed, incorporating details and elaboration that support and extend the main idea of the piece. It should show that these students can use literary strategies—anecdotes and repetition, for example—to develop their ideas. At the same time, the writing should be well crafted, organized, and coherent, and it should incorporate techniques such as a consistency in topic or theme, sequencing, and a clear introduction and conclusion. It should show that these writers can engage the audience they are expected to address through rich and compelling language, precise word choice, and variety in sentence structure. Writing by twelfth-grade students performing at the Advanced level should contain few errors in grammar, spelling, punctuation, capitalization, and sentence structure. (Excerpted from Persky, Daane, and Jin 2003, 11).

- teacher discussions about desired skills and the development of a scope and sequence of writing skills that are supported in content-area classes as well as in language arts classes;

- opportunities for content-area teachers to work with language arts teachers for assistance on how to help students address their most common writing problems;

- the development of schoolwide rubrics of what constitutes effective writing—with students and teachers knowledgeable of these and with the rubrics consistently used to assess student work; and

- professional development opportunities focused on writing for teachers who received little preservice training on the teaching of writing.

The Jefferson County, Ky. Public School District has engaged in a focused effort to help all teachers support the development of student writing skills. In collaboration with the Kentucky Department of Education, the district has developed a series of marker papers to guide teachers in their assessment of student writing. The marker papers are a collection of examples of proficient students' writing. As a set, the marker papers "illustrate the progression of key writing skills in specific types of writing" (Collaborative Communications Group 2001, online). Each paper also is annotated to highlight the specific skills the writer has demonstrated.

According to state and county officials, the "papers help teachers see that one lesson will not suit all kids because there is a continuum of developmental levels in students' writing ability" (Collaborative Communications Group 2001). When teachers compare a student's work against the marker papers, they are able to see where the students is on the proficiency continuum and what the student needs to learn next. Suggestions for subsequent lessons are included on the marker papers to help teachers with their planning.

Teachers in the district often look together at student work and then compare the marker papers for their grade level against the work of individual students. By doing this, they are able to discuss the developments they see in student writing—a conversation that often aids their own understanding of how students learn to write. This approach, including collaborative work to develop rubrics and time for teachers to review and discuss student work from the perspective of these rubrics, could be used at an individual school.

Merritt suggests schools also consider "discussing and establishing a consistent marking system" (2003, 38) to be used in all classes to support students as they engage in writing. For example, an "*" could mean "say more here" and a "?" could mean "this puzzles me" (Strong 2001). This consistency in teacher response helps students struggling with writing to focus on real issues instead of on efforts to "figure out" what a particular teacher means.

Carter suggests teachers be provided with some general questions to use when reviewing and responding to student writing. Questions such as these could be incorporated in rubrics or used in addition to them; for example:

1) Did the writer show signs of creativity?

2) Did the writer organize thoughts in a useful way (chronological, topical)?

3) Did the writer begin the assignment with an interesting, logical lead-in?

4) Did the writer close his or her piece with a clincher idea?

5) Do you think the essay/poem/story is representative of the time given to complete the assignment?

6) Did the writer appear to have a grasp of grammatical and syntactical skills? (1991, 347).

School leaders also are in a position to use parents as resources in helping students develop as writers. For example, the Lake Washington School District (Wash.) (2001) has published—and makes available through its Web site—*The 6+1 Traits of Effective Writing: Handbook for High School Parents* (www.lkwash.wednet.edu/lwsd/pdf/6+1Traits.pdf). In addition to describing the 6+1 Traits writing model, the handbook includes information on ways parents can help students develop as writers. For example, in a section titled "How can I help my student with the writing process?," parents are advised in the section on drafting not to write for your student but to answer questions about word choice, ideas, and content.

The National Commission on Writing in America's Schools and Colleges highlights the importance of the development of student writing skills. In its view, "The reward of disciplined writing is the most valuable job attribute of all: a mind equipped to think. Writing today is not a frill for the few, but an essential skill for the many" (2003, online).

Although the instructional days in middle and high schools are jam-packed with content that must be taught, it is important that writing instruction not be short-changed. By developing a schoolwide focus on the teaching of writing—and by providing teachers with the training and support they need to embed the teaching of writing in content-area classes—schools can ensure students leave with the skills they need to succeed to enter high school, college, and the workforce. Just as important, opportunities to write across the curriculum can help students to develop critical thinking skills and to understand key concepts and connections in content areas.

References

Ameig, T.M. (1993). Learning the language of music through journals. *Music Educators Journal* (January 1993), 30-32.

American Council on Education. (1999). *Alignment of national and state standards: A report by the GED Testing Service.* Washington, DC: Author.

Andrews, S.E. (1997). Writing to learn in content area reading class. *Journal of Adolescent and Adult Literacy* (October 1997), 141-142.

Atwell, N. (1998). *In the middle: Writing, reading, and learning with adolescents.* Portsmouth, NH: Heinemann.

Bagley, T., & Gallenberger, C. (1992). Assessing students' dispositions: Using journals to improve students' performance. *The Mathematics Teacher* (November 1992), 660-663.

Birnbaum, J.C. (1986). Reflective thought: The connection between reading and writing. In B.T. Petersen (Ed.), *Convergences: Transactions in reading and writing* (pp. 30-45). Urbana, IL: National Council of Teachers of English.

Boise State Writing Center. (2003). Getting a draft written. *Word Works: Learning Through Writing at Boise State University* (February 2003). Retrieved from http://www.boisestate.edu/wcenter/ww119.htm

Boss, S. (2002). Everybody writes: English language learners discover their voice. *Northwest Education* (Winter 2002), 17-19.

Brostoff, A. (1979). Good assignments lead to good writing. *Social Education* (March 1979), 184-186.

Burns, M. (1995). Writing in math class? Absolutely! *Instructor* (April 1995), 40-47.

Carter, J.M. (1991). The social studies teacher as writing coach. *The Clearing House* (May/June 1991), 346-349.

Cochran, J.A. (1993). *Reading in the content areas for junior high and high school.* Boston: Allyn and Bacon.

Collaborative Communications Group. (2001). *Marker papers: A tool for teachers to evaluate their students' writing and to plan and improve their own writing instruction.* Retrieved from http://www.publicengagement.com/resources/standards/oldstandards/assessing/as_markerpapers.htm

College Board, The. (n.d.). *The new SAT 2005.* Retrieved from http://www.collegeboard.com/newsat/hs/hs.html

Composition Center of Dartmouth College. (n.d.). *The process approach to teaching writing.* Retrieved from http://www.dartmouth.edu/~compose/tutor/pedagogy/process.html

Countryman, J. (2001). Writing to learn mathematics. *ENC Online.* Retrieved from http://www.enc.org/features/focus/archive/across/document.shtm?input=FOC-002775-index

Crowley, M.L. (1993). Student mathematics portfolio: More than a display case. *The Mathematics Teacher, 86*(7), 544-547.

Farr, R. (1993). Writing in response to reading: A process approach to literacy assessment. In B.E. Cullinan (Ed.), *Pen in hand: Children become writers* (pp. 64-79). Newark, DE: International Reading Association.

Fitzgerald, J. (1989). Enhancing two related thought processes: Revision in writing and critical reading. *The Reading Teacher, 43*, 42-48.

Fuhler, C.J. (1994). Response journals: Just one more time with feeling. *Journal of Reading, 37*(5), 400-405.

Goldsby, D.S., & Cozza, B. (2002). Writing samples to understand mathematical thinking. *Mathematics Teaching in the Middle School* (May 2002), 517-520.

Graham, S. (1992). Helping students with LD progress as writers. *Intervention in School and Clinic* (January 1992), 134-144.

Graham, S., & Harris, K.R. (1999). Assessment and intervention in overcoming writing difficulties: An illustration from the self-regulated strategy development model. *Language, Speech, and Hearing Services in Schools* (July 1999), 255-264.

Gross, P.A. (1992, December). *Shared meaning: Whole language reader response at the secondary level*. Paper presented at the annual meeting of the National Reading Conference, San Antonio, TX. ERIC Document No. 359 491.

Gunning, T.G. (2003). *Building literacy in the content areas*. Boston: Allyn & Bacon.

Gutman, L.E., & Sulzby, E. (2001). *The role of autonomy-support versus control in the emergent writing behaviors of African American kindergarten children*. Retrieved from http://www.ciera.org/library/archive/2000-03/art-online-00-03.html

Hickey, M.G. (1990). Reading and social studies: The critical connection. *Social Education, 33*(7), 175-176.

Hiebert, E.H. (1991). Literacy contexts and literacy processes. *Language Arts, 68*(2), 134-139.

Hopkins, G. (1999). Journal writing every day: Teachers say it really works! *Education World* (June 7, 1999). Retrieved from http://www.education-world.com/a_curr/curr144.shtml

Isaacson, S. (1991). Written expression and the challenges for students with learning problems. *Exceptionality Education Canada, 1*(3), 45-57.

Jacobs, V.A. (2002). Reading, writing, and understanding. *Educational Leadership* (November 2002), 58-61.

Johnson, J., Holcombe, M., Simms, G., & Wilson, D. (1993). Writing to learn in a content area. *The Clearing House* (January/February 1993), 155-158.

Jones, R.C. (2001). Strategies for reading comprehension: Reciprocal teaching. *ReadingQuest.org: Making Sense of Social Studies*. Retrieved from http://curry.edschool.virginia.edu/go/readquest/strat/rt.html

Kenyon, R.W. (2000). Using writing in mathematics. In D. Worsley & B. Mayer (Eds.). *The Art of Science Writing* (pp. 199-206). New York: Teachers and Writers Collaborative.

Klingner, J.K., & Vaughn, S. (1998). Using collaborative strategic reading. *Teaching Exceptional Children* (July/August 1998), 32-37.

Knudson, R.E. (1989). *Teaching children to write: Informal writing*. ERIC Document Reproduction Service No. ED310425.

Kroll, L., & Halaby, M. (1997). Writing to learn mathematics in the primary school. *Young Children* (May 1997), 54-59.

Langer, J.A., with Close, E., Angelis, J., & Preller, P. (2000). *Guidelines for teaching middle and high school students to read and write well: Six features of effective instruction*. Albany, NY: National Research Center on English Learning and Achievement.

Langer, J., & Flihan, S. (2000). *Writing and reading relationships: Constructive tasks*. Retrieved from http://cela.albany.edu/publication/article/writeread.htm

Marchisan, M.L., & Alber, S.R. (2001). The write way: Tips for teaching the writing process to resistant writers. *Intervention in School and Clinic* (January 2001), 154-162.

Maryland Department of Education. (n.d.). *What have we learned about good instruction: Thinking skills and writing*. Retrieved from http://www.mdk12.org/instruction/success%5Fmspap/general/projectbetter/social/ss%2D63%2D64.html

Merritt, S.P. (2003). *Writing across the curriculum: High school teachers handbook*. Raleigh, NC: Pubic Schools of North Carolina, Department of Public Instruction. Retrieved from http://www.ncpublicschools.org/curriculum/languagearts/resources/writing/writinghandbook.pdf

Mitchell, D. (1996). Writing to learn across the curriculum and the English teacher. *English Journal* (September 1996), 93-97.

Montague, M., & Leavell, A.G. (1994). Improving the narrative writing of students with learning disabilities. *Remedial and Special Education* (January 1994), 21-33.

Murray, D.M. (2002). *Write to learn*. Boston: Thomson Learning, Inc.

National Commission on Writing in America's Schools and Colleges. (2003). *The neglected "R": The need for a writing revolution*. New York: The College Board. Retrieved from http://www.writingcommission.org/prod_downloads/writingcom/neglectedr.pdf

National Council of Teachers of Mathematics. (2000). *Principles and standards for school mathematics*. Reston, VA: Author. Retrieved from http://standards.nctm.org/document/index.htm

National Science Resources Center. (2001). Writing in the science classroom: Essential for many reasons. *ScienceLink* (Fall/Winter 2001). Retrieved from http://www.si.edu/nsrc/pubs/newsletter/Fall-Winter%202001/Writing%20in%20the%20Science%20Classroom.htm

North Carolina Department of Public Instruction Testing Section. (2003). *Understanding the North Carolina writing assessment scoring model at grades 4, 7, & 10*. Raleigh, NC: Author. Retrieved from http://www.ncpublicschools.org/accountability/testing/writing/July%20Scoring%20Criteria.pdf

Northwest Regional Educational Laboratory. (n.d.). *6+1 trait writing assessment scoring guide*. Retrieved from http://www.nwrel.org/assessment/pdfRubrics/6plus1traits

Northwest Regional Educational Laboratory. (2001). *6+1 trait writing*. Retrieved from http://www.nwrel.org/assessment/department.asp?d=1

Oldfather, P. (1995). Commentary: What's needed to maintain and extend motivation for literacy instruction in the middle grades? *Journal of Reading*, 38, 420-422.

Persky, H.R., Daane, M.C., & Jin, Y. (2003). *The nation's report card: Writing 2002*. Washington, DC: U.S. Department of Education. Institute of Education Sciences. National Center for Education Statistics. Retrieved from http://nces.ed.gov/nationsreportcard/pdf/main2002/2003529.pdf

Peterson, A. (2001). NAEP/NWP study shows link between assignments, better student writing. *The Voice* (March-April 2001). Retrieved from http:// www.writingproject.org/pub/nwpr/ voice/2001no2/peterson.html

Pugalee, D.K. (1997). Connecting writing to the mathematics curriculum. *The Mathematics Teacher* (April 1997), 308-310.

Pugalee, D.K., DiBiase, W.J., & Wood, K.D. (1999). Writing and the development of problem solving in mathematics and science. *Middle School Journal* (May 1999), 48-52.

Raphael, T.E., & Englert, C.S. (1990). Writing and reading: Partners in constructing meaning. *The Reading Teacher, 43*(6), 388-400.

Reed, B. (2002). Learning by the book: Students publish a series of local bestsellers. *Northwest Education* (Winter 2002), 22-24.

Reid, L. (1983, Spring). *Talking: The neglected part of the writing process*. Paper presented at the annual meeting of the National Council of Teachers of English, Seattle, WA.

Rhodes, L.K., & Dudley-Marling, C. (1996). *Readers and writers with a difference* (2nd ed.). Portsmouth, NH: Heinemann.

Risinger, C.F. (1987). Improving writing skills through social studies. *ERIC Digest*. Bloomington, IN: ERIC Clearinghouse for Social Studies/Social Science Education. Retrieved from http:// www.ericfacility.net/databases/ERIC_Digests/ed285829.html

Ross, C.L. (1998). Journaling across the curriculum. *The Clearing House* (January/February 1998), 189-190.

Roush, N.M. (1992). The collaborative approach to writing. *Gifted Child Today* (September/ October 1992), 29-31.

Routmann, R. (1996). *Literacy at the crossroads: Critical talk about reading, writing, and other teaching dilemmas*. Portsmouth, NH: Heinemann.

Russek, B. (1998). Writing to learn mathematics. *Writing Across the Curriculum* (August 1998), 36-45.

Savage, J.F. (1998). *Teaching reading and writing: Combining skills, strategies, and literature*. Boston: McGraw-Hill.

Scala, M.C. (2001). *Working together: Reading and writing in inclusive classrooms*. Newark, DE: International Reading Association.

Simic, M. (1994). Computer assisted writing instruction. *ERIC Digest*. ERIC Clearinghouse on Reading, English, and Communication. Retrieved from http://www.indiana.edu/~eric_rec/ ieo/digests/d97.html

Smith, C.B., & Dahl, K.L. (1984). *Teaching reading and writing together: The classroom connection*. New York: Teachers College Press.

Song, M. (1998). *Experimental study of the effect of controlled vs. freewriting and different feedback types on writing quality and writing apprehension of EFL college students.* South Korea. ERIC Document Reproduction Service No. ED423703.

Sorenson, S. (1991). Encouraging writing achievement: Writing across the curriculum. *ERIC Digest.* Bloomington, IN: ERIC Clearinghouse on Reading and Communication Skills. Retrieved from http://www.ericfacility.net/ericdigests/ed327879.html

Stein, M., Dixon, R., & Barnard, S. (2001). What research tells us about writing instruction for students in the middle grades. *Journal of Direct Instruction* (Summer 2001), 107-116.

Stephens, E.C., & Brown, J.E. (2000). *A handbook of content literacy strategies: 75 practical reading and writing ideas.* Norwood, MA: Christopher-Gordon Publishers, Inc.

Stotsky, S. (1994). Connecting writing and reading with a civic twist. *The Reading Teacher* (October 1994), 172-174.

Strange, R.L. (1988). Audience awareness: When and how does it develop? *ERIC Digest No. 29.* ERIC Clearinghouse on Reading, English, and Communication. Retrieved from http://www.indiana.edu/~eric_rec/ieo/digests/d29.html

Strickland, D.S., & Morrow, L.M. (Eds.). (2000). *Beginning reading and writing.* Newark, DE: International Reading Association and New York: Teachers College Press.

Strickland, D.S., Ganske, K., & Monroe, J.K. (2002). *Supporting struggling readers and writers: Strategies for classroom intervention.* Portland, ME: Stenhouse Publishers and Newark, DE: International Reading Association.

Strong, W. (2001). *Coaching writing: The power of guided practice.* Portsmouth, NH: Heinemann.

Strong, R.W., Silver, H.F., Perini, M.J., & Tuculescu, G.M. (2002). *Reading for academic success: Powerful strategies for struggling, average, and advanced readers, grades 7-12.* Thousand Oaks, CA: Corwin Press, Inc.

Teale, W.H., & Yakota, J. (2000). Beginning reading and writing: Perspectives on instruction. In D.S. Strickland & L.M. Morrow (Eds.), *Beginning reading and writing* (pp. 3-22). New York: Teachers College Press and Newark, DE: International Reading Association.

Texas Center for Reading and Language Arts. (2000). *Professional development guide: Enhancing writing instruction for secondary students.* Austin, TX: Author. Retrieved from http://readingserver.edb.utexas.edu/downloads/special_ed/secondaryoriginal/2000_writing_inst_SE.pdf

Tierney, R.J., & Leys, M. (1986). What is the value of connecting reading and writing? In B.T. Petersen (Ed.), *Convergences: Transactions in reading and writing* (pp. 15-29). Urbana, IL: National Council of Teachers of English.

Tompkins, G.E. (1998). *Language arts: Content and teaching strategies* (4th ed.). Upper Saddle River, NJ: Prentice-Hall, Inc.

Tuley, S.L. (1994). Creative testing: Hamlet, Celie, and Gulliver rendezvous in a final exam. *English Journal, 83*(8), 77-80.

University of Texas Center for Reading & Language Arts. (2003). *Enhancing learning through reading and writing strategies in the content areas (revised).* Austin, TX: Author. Retrieved from http://readingserver.edb.utexas.edu/downloads/secondary/guides 2003ContentArea_bw.pdf

Veit, R. (1981). *Creating conditions for learning: A further argument for free writing*. Paper presented at the annual meeting of the Conference on College Composition and Communication, Dallas, TX.

Ventre, R. (1979). Developmental writing: Social studies assignments. *Social Education* (March 1979), 181-183, 197.

Vermont Business Roundtable. (1995). *What do employers expect . . . from today's high school graduates?* South Burlington, VT: Author. Retrieved from http://www.vtroundtable.org/siteimages/Whatdoem.pdf

WAC Clearinghouse, Colorado State University. *An introduction to WAC: Examples of writing to learn activities*. (n.d.). Fort Collins, CO: Author. Retrieved from http://wac.colostate.edu/intro/pop5.cfm

Walberg, H.J, & Paik, S.J. (2004). Effective general practices. In G. Cawelti (Ed.), *Handbook of Research on Improving Student Achievement* (3rd ed.), pp. 25-38. Arlington, VA: Educational Research Service.

Walley, C., & Kommer, D. (2000). Writing as part of the team. *The Clearing House* (March/April 2000), 232-234.

Warger, C. (2002). Helping students with disabilities succeed in state and district writing assessments *(ERIC/OSEP Digest ED463622)*. Arlington, VA: ERIC Clearinghouse on Disabilities and Gifted Education. Retrieved from http://iris.peabody.vanderbilt.edu/info_briefs/eric/ericdigest/ed463622.html

Weber, A. (2000). Playful writing for critical thinking: Four approaches to writing. *Journal of Adolescent and Adult Literacy* (March 2000), 562-568.

Wells, M.C. (1993). At the junction of reading and writing: How dialogue journals contribute to students' reading development. *Journal of Reading, 36*(4), 294-302.

Wildeman, J. (1988). *Defining audience negatively: One way that writers keep readers from their texts*. Paper presented at the 39th annual meeting of the Conference on College Composition and Communication.

Williams, A.P. (1992). *A comparison between the reading comprehension of eleventh grade students who incorporate free writing exercises into their literature class and those eleventh grade students who do not incorporate free writing into their literature class*. McKeesport, PA: McKeesport Area School District.

Wisconsin Department of Public Instruction. (1998). District writing assessment. In *Wisconsin Model Academic Standards for English Language Arts*. Retrieved from http://www.dpi.state.wi.us/dpi/standards/elaintro.html

Wittrock, C.A., & Barrow, L.H. (2000). Blow-by-blow inquiry. *Science and Children* (February 2000), 34-38.

Wood, K., & Shea-Bischoff, P. (1997). Helping struggling writers write. *Middle School Journal* (March 1997), 50-53.

Index

A

Admit/Exit Slips 37

Anticipation Guides 52

Assessment 2, 33, 67, 68, 69, 71, 74, 92, 94, 95, 96

Audience 2, 3, 17, 19, 20, 21, 23, 24, 29, 30, 35, 42, 44, 64, 72, 73, 79, 82, 86, 88, 92, 94, 96

B

Beginning Writing 10, 11

Brainstorm 12, 24, 28, 29, 36, 53, 80, 84

Bumper Stickers 53

C

Clay 8

Collaboration 14, 15, 95

Collaborative learning 50

Conventional spelling 11

Conventions 3, 11, 12, 18, 23, 73, 80, 87

Cooperative Learning 13, 50

Criteria Charts 74

Crossword Puzzles 52

D

Dialogue Journals 42, 43

Drafting 17, 18, 22, 24, 53, 97

E

Editing 2, 8, 18, 22, 24, 25, 26, 68, 86

Elaboration 23, 92, 94, 96

Emergent Literacy 8, 9

Emergent Writing 10, 11

English Language Arts Standards 3

F

Fluent Writing 10, 12, 86

Focus 1, 2, 11, 12, 18, 23, 24, 25, 29, 31, 36, 37, 39, 40, 46, 47, 51, 52, 63, 64, 71, 73, 74, 76, 79, 82, 85, 87, 95, 97, 98

Free-write 6, 36, 37

G

Godoy-Gonzalez 62

Grammar 6, 15, 30, 39, 41, 42, 43, 60, 73, 75, 76, 85, 87, 88, 92, 94, 96

H

Handwriting 17, 24

Hot Cards 52

I

Inquiry-based learning 61

Integrate 6, 8, 20, 30, 35, 80

Integration 3, 57

Invented spelling 9, 11

J

Jefferson County 95

Journal Writing 38, 39, 40, 41, 42, 50, 58, 69

K

"Kid" writing 12

L

Learning Logs 45, 48

Literature 5, 12, 24, 26, 27, 39

M

McKay 14, 15

Mechanics of Writing 24, 30, 31, 85

Merritt 13, 14, 17, 18, 21, 27, 37, 50, 53, 87, 97

Metacognition 48

Metacognitive awareness 7

Metaphors 53

Morrow 70

Motivation 12, 13, 14, 15, 17, 20, 22, 45, 48

Murray 11

N

NAEP 20, 92, 94, 96

National Assessment of Educational Progress 2

National Commission on Writing in America's School 2, 3, 33, 97

National Council of Teachers of Mathematics 57

Northwest Regional Educational Laboratory 71, 73

O

Organization 20, 23, 65, 71, 73, 75, 79, 84, 85, 86, 109

P

Peer response 87

Phonics 9

Picture books 82, 83

Playful Writing 83

Previewing Text 36

Prewriting 18, 22, 24, 36, 37, 53, 82, 85

Prior knowledge 37, 39, 53, 63, 64

Process approach 6, 17, 22, 26

Professional development 6, 7, 95

Proofreading 31

Publishing 15, 18, 22, 26

Punctuation 6, 11, 17, 24, 26, 30, 31, 39, 42, 59, 73, 92, 94, 96

Purpose 2, 3, 5, 10, 17, 21, 23, 26, 27, 29, 35, 38, 39, 46, 67, 68, 72, 73, 79, 80, 82, 84, 88, 92, 96

R

Read aloud 24

Reading aloud 11, 51, 85

Reading and Writing as Interrelated Processes 9

Reading-writing connection 10

Reciprocal Teaching Journals 44

Reflective writing 48, 50

Revising 2, 6, 10, 17, 18, 22, 24, 26, 36, 62, 85, 86, 88

Revision 2, 18, 24, 85, 86, 87, 88, 89

Rubrics 68, 71, 73, 74, 95, 97

S

6+1 Traits of Student Writing 71

Scaffolding 14, 20

Self-evaluation checklist 86

Sentence fluency 23, 72

Shared reading 11

Shea-Bischoff 80, 82

Snapshot summaries 50

Standards 1, 3, 14, 15, 57, 80, 92

Standards for writing 1

Strickland 14, 67, 70, 76, 77

Strong 1, 5, 7, 15, 20, 40, 48, 50, 51, 52, 58, 62, 63, 72, 83, 85, 88, 97

Struggling writers 6, 10, 79, 80, 85

Student-student conferences 25

Style 12, 17, 23, 24, 29, 43, 53, 59, 73, 86

Sulzby 9, 12

T

Teale 9

Technology 14, 61, 85, 86

Telegrams 52

Think-Pair-Share 50

Tompkins 9, 10, 11, 12, 30, 31, 39

Topic 2, 6, 12, 13, 17, 21, 23, 24, 25, 26, 27, 28, 29, 30, 33, 35, 36, 37, 38, 47, 48, 50, 52, 53, 59, 63, 64, 71, 72, 79, 82, 83, 84, 85, 86, 88, 94, 96, 97

Trade books 24

V

Venn Diagrams 52

Voice 38, 50, 62, 64, 71, 72, 76, 82

W

Wood 61, 80, 82

Word choice 23, 24, 72, 92, 94, 97

writing across the curriculum 33, 98

Writing in mathematics 57, 58

Writing in science 13, 61

Writing in social studies 5, 62

Writing process 3, 15, 18, 22, 24, 25, 26, 35, 40, 61, 76, 82, 86, 97

Writing prompts 27

Writing to learn 33, 34, 46, 52, 54, 55, 91

NOTES

ORDER FORM FOR RELATED RESOURCES

Quantity	Item # and Title	Price Per Item			Total Price
		Base Price	ERS Individual Subscriber Discount Price	ERS School District Subscriber Discount Price	
	What We Know About: Writing Across the Curriculum to Increase Student Learning in Middle and High School (#0558)	$20	$15	$10	
	What We Know About: Reading at the Middle and High School Levels, 3rd Edition (#0536)	$20	$15	$10	
	What We Know About: Helping Middle and High School Readers (#0448)	$18	$13.50	$9	
Single copy only	*ERS Info-File Writing Across the Curriculum* (#5207)	$40	$30	$20	

Postage and Handling ** (Add the greater of $4.50 or 10% of purchase price.):	
** Please double for international orders.	**Express Delivery ** (Add $20 for second-business-day service.):**
	TOTAL DUE:

SATISFACTION GUARANTEED!
If you are not satisfied with an ERS resource, return it in its original condition within 30 days of receipt and we will give you a full refund.

Method of payment:

❑ Check enclosed (payable to Educational Research Service).

❑ Purchase order enclosed. (P.O.#_____)

Bill my: ❑ VISA ❑ MasterCard ❑ American Express

Visit us online at www.ers.org for a complete listing of resources!

Name on Card (print)

Account Number _____ Expiration Date _____

Signature _____ Date _____

Shipping address:

❑ Dr. ❑ Mr. ❑ Mrs. ❑ Ms.   Name

Position _____ ERS Subscriber ID#

School District or Agency

Street Address

City _____ State _____ Zip

Phone _____ Fax _____ Email

Return completed order form to: Educational Research Service
1001 North Fairfax Street, Alexandria, VA 22314-1587
Phone: (800) 791-9308 • Fax: (800) 791-9309 • Email: ers@ers.org • Web site: www.ers.org

If you are looking for reliable K-12 research to . . .

- identify research-based teaching practices;

- make educationally sound and cost-effective decisions; and most importantly

- improve student achievement . . .

then you need look no further than an ERS Subscription.

Simply choose the subscription option that best meets your needs:

✓ **School District Subscription**—a special research and information subscription that provides education leaders with timely research on priority issues in K-12 education. All new ERS publications and periodicals, access to customized information services through the ERS special library, and 50 percent discounts on additional ERS resources are included in this subscription for one annual fee. This subscription also provides the entire administrative staff "instant" online, searchable access to the wide variety of ERS resources. You'll gain access to the ERS electronic library of more than 1,600 educational research-based documents, as well as additional content uploaded throughout the year.

✓ **Individual Subscription**—designed primarily for school administrators, staff, and school board members who want to receive a personal copy of new ERS studies, reports, and/or periodicals published and special discounts on other resources purchased.

✓ **Other Education Agency Subscription**—available for state associations, libraries, departments of education, service centers, and other organizations needing access to quality research and information resources and services.

Your ERS Subscription benefits begin as soon as your order is received and continue for 12 months. For more detailed subscription information and pricing, contact ERS toll free at (800) 791-9308, by email at ers@ers.org, or visit us online at www.ers.org!